Pink

IS THE NEW BLACK

Pink

IS THE NEW BLACK

SARAH MCLEAN

Pink Is the New Black
Copyright © 2015 by Sarah McLean

ISBN: 978-0-9980004-0-4

Editor: David Lambert
Photo Credit: Randy Coleman Photography
Cover Design: Shane Brock
Interior Design: Anne Huizenga

Printed in the United States of America

15 16 17 18 19 20 21 • 10 9 8 7 6 5 4 3 2 1

Dedication

This book is dedicated to my husband, Steve—my life-partner and biggest cheerleader and fan. Steve, without your support, dedication, enduring love, and perseverance, I wouldn't have been able to make it through the many battles we've endured. Thank you! I love you!

Contents

Foreword

Even though I walk through the darkest valley,
I will fear no evil, for you are with me; your
rod and your staff, they comfort me.

Psalm 23:4 NIV

Without faith, our natural reaction to dark valleys is
fear. We isolate ourselves and cower in the darkness,
not knowing what to do or where to turn. But when we
put our faith in God, we learn that he is there to love us,
comfort us, fight for us, and give us hope and a purpose
in the midst of our pain.

When I was five years old, a cancer diagnosis led to the
removal of my right eye. I remember feeling so violated,
feeling that something precious had been stolen from
me without my consent. It would be many years before
I met the Lord and was able to release all the fear and
anger to which that experience had left me bound. But
through him, I was able to turn my experiences around
and have an impact on more lives than I ever could have
imagined.

Scripture tells us:

Therefore we do not lose heart. Though
outwardly we are wasting away, yet inwardly
we are being renewed day by day. For our
light and momentary troubles are achieving for
us an eternal glory that far outweighs them all.

(2 Corinthians 4:16–17 NIV)

Sarah's story has deeply impacted me. I am amazed by her faith and resilience in light of all she has endured. She has grieved, but she has also decided to believe that God has a plan even in the midst of her pain.

It would have been easy for Sarah to deny God's goodness and turn away from him. Instead, she turned her gaze upward and outward, recognizing that her momentary troubles were going to bring a greater glory. She learned, too, that the God who stayed with her through her pain longs to draw near to others going through similar trials. That knowledge is helping her bring hope and encouragement to many.

Writing this book is one more bold action of love Sarah has taken to offer strength and healing to the hurting. I am so proud of her, and I know there will be an eternal ripple effect resulting from her courage. As you read her story, may you be encouraged, uplifted, and inspired!

> He comforts us in all our troubles so that we can comfort others. When they are troubled, we will be able to give them the same comfort God has given us.
> (2 Corinthians 1:4 NLT)

Lisa Bevere
Messenger International
Best-Selling Author of
Lioness Arising, Kissed the Girls and Made Them Cry,
and *Fight Like a Girl*

Acknowledgments

My Family—Steve, Colin, and Tatum
I thank my family for being my biggest cheerleaders. Without your love and support, I wouldn't have been able to walk through this journey. Thank you for being patient with me and giving me the grace to accomplish a major life goal: becoming a published author. I love you!

Dave Lambert
Thank you to Dave Lambert. You've been my editor, encourager, and coach through the past year and a half. From the very beginning of this process, I've been scared to tackle such an emotionally challenging project, but you have given me direction, counsel, and the courage to keep going. You're a godsend!

Somersault Team—Jeannette Taylor,
Cindy Lambert, and Joe Sherman
Thank you, guys, for being my guiding light throughout this process. You've given me the strength and confidence to share my story with the world. Because of your wisdom and leadership, I believe women's lives will be forever changed!

Project31 Board—Jane Wilson, Dawn Harth,
Caitlin Grassmyer, Melissa Craft, Michelle Garrett,
and Nick Brown
You're only as strong as the team you put around you. My board has been by my side every step of the way. Thank you for your support and your belief in our vision!

Craig Groeschel

I was Craig's personal assistant for over eight years. Thank you, Craig, for your leadership, integrity, and passion and for never allowing fear to get in the way of accomplishing your dreams. You've been a tremendous example to me to swing for the fence!

Lisa Bevere

You are a "spiritual mother" to so many women. Thank you for investing in and believing in me. Your passion, strength, and sass are intoxicating. I want to be you when I grow up!

Joanna and Michael "Smitty" Smith

Thank you for believing in me! Your investment in my development has been life changing. Without your guidance, insight, and willingness to take a chance on me, I wouldn't be where I am today!

Chapter One
This Can't Be Happening

Well, that's new, I thought. Hot water splashed down my back, and the smell of eucalyptus body wash filled the steamy air. The morning news on the *Today Show* from the TV in our bedroom mumbled faintly.

It was a cool morning in November of 2002. I stood in the shower of our new apartment in Oklahoma City, doing a breast exam. With my right arm resting on my head, I gently pressed the fingertips of my left hand against the tissue throughout the area of my right breast, from collarbone to armpit. I knew exactly what my tissue should feel like because I'd been doing self-exams regularly for seven years—since I'd turned eighteen and my doctor had encouraged them and taught me to do them the right way. They were surprisingly easy, and doing them gave me a sense of empowerment over my own health. I did them faithfully—even though, honestly, I didn't think I really needed them. My chest was so small— barely an "A" cup. I'd always thought that women with fuller breasts were more susceptible to cancer

> A chill of worry washed over me.
> Should I be concerned about this?
> Surely it wasn't cancer.

and other related illnesses. In fact, I thought it would be practically impossible for me to get breast cancer.

That morning, I explored the area as I always did—with my mind mostly on the day's activities. But this time was different. My fingertips told me that something had changed. My mind abruptly forgot about making my to-do list and paid attention. I paused, then my fingers inspected the area just above my nipple again with deeper pressure, and again with even deeper pressure. I thought I felt something there—a change from normal. But I wasn't sure. A chill of worry washed over me. Should I be concerned about this? Surely it wasn't cancer.

I shrugged it off and reached for the shampoo. Whatever this was, it couldn't be anything serious—I was too young. *Twenty-five-year-old women don't get breast cancer*, I told myself, pushing aside that twinge of anxiety. No point in worrying over nothing, right?

I rinsed my hair and finished bathing. I turned off the water and stepped out of the shower onto the bathmat. After drying off, I wiped the steam off the mirror and wrapped myself in my towel. I stood in front of the mirror, gazing at myself and thinking,

What would you do if you had cancer? How would that change your life?

"Babe, would you like some coffee?" my husband, Steve, called from the kitchen.

I snapped out of it. "That would be great. Thank you." I said.

As I put on my makeup and fixed my hair, I couldn't shake the sense of unease. *There's no history of breast cancer in our family. I'm young. I'm healthy.*

I grabbed my purse, hot coffee, and laptop, and then gave Steve a kiss and told him to have a good day. I closed the door behind me—time to get on with the day.

And get on with it I did. And with the next day, and the day after that, and before I knew it four months had gone by, and I'd done nothing about the "lump" I'd found.

In March of 2003, my gynecologist—a new one a friend had recommended—led me through a routine appointment, just like the one all women check off their to-do list at some point each year. While she finished her paperwork in silence, I sat apprehensively, trying to distract myself by reviewing her diploma on the wall, the plastic models of body parts on her counter, the posters encouraging patients to do breast exams and get yearly checkups. When she was finished, she smiled, sat back, and said, "I don't think you have anything to be worried about."

Odd how much relief I felt hearing her say it, even though that's exactly what I'd expected her to say. Since discovering the unusual tissue a few months before, I had continued my monthly breast exams but felt a subtle and growing uneasiness as I noticed gradual changes in that little spot in my right breast. Within a couple of months, I'd had to admit: It was clearly a lump. But I was still convinced I was too young to have anything to worry about. I was healthy and working hard at a job I loved. Steve and I were talking about starting our family. Our lives were full of activity and bustling with career growth. We had plans for the future. There was no place in our life for cancer. So I had just quieted the little voice within me and continued about the business of life.

"You say the lump is a bit sensitive?" the gynecologist continued.

"A little," I said, allowing the apprehension and uncertainty to show through my voice.

Seeing my worry, she assured me, "That's good, actually. Cysts are fairly common and can be sensitive to the touch. Cancer is generally free of sensation—that's one reason people may not detect it. Besides, I'd have been very surprised to see breast cancer in someone as young as you are."

"That's what I thought," I said, a gasp of relief escaping between my words.

She was so matter-of-fact with her assessment, so confidently dismissive, that I left her office feeling slightly embarrassed that I had wasted energy worrying over something so minute. But I was also relieved that my assumption had been affirmed: I was too young for breast cancer, and there was nothing to be concerned about.

Over the next months, my self-exams revealed that the lump was continuing to grow, and it became even more tender to the touch. In fact, it reached the point that, whenever I examined the area, I felt twinges of pain.

Was this normal? A good sign? Bad? I didn't know anyone who had breast cancer I could ask, so I decided to do some research online. My research confirmed what the doctor had said: Cysts hurt and cancer doesn't. I tried to convince myself I had nothing to worry about as a way of stuffing my growing concern.

Even so, because of the changes in the lump, Steve insisted I go back to the doctor for another look. It had been a couple of months since my initial visit, and at least six months since I found the lump in the shower. So I made a follow-up appointment with the same doctor. I asked Steve to come with me this time.

With soft instrumental music in the background, Steve and I sat in the waiting room watching the nurse escort patient after patient in and out. I scanned the room, wondering what each woman was there for. In the corner a woman and her husband whispered quietly as they held hands waiting for their name to be called. On the other side of the room an elderly lady sat flipping the pages of a women's magazine. *Were they scared like me?* The longer we waited, the sillier I felt. I thought, *Why am I here? This is nothing. She's already examined me once and assured me nothing was wrong. She's a professional. She knows what cancer feels like. But … what if this is something more than a cyst?*

"Sarah." Hearing the nurse call my name filled me with a mixed sense of relief and dread.

She escorted Steve and me back to an examining room. "Take everything off from the waist up," she said. "Put the gown on with the opening in front. The doctor will be in shortly."

"Thank you," I said.

When the doctor entered, I was sitting on the examining table, anxious, tightly holding together the opening in the gown. She seemed cold and unsympathetic. Maybe she was overworked or having a bad day, but she didn't exude any feelings of compassion or concern. Her body language was stiff, and she seemed to be in a hurry. I got the impression that she thought I was making a big deal out of nothing, and she didn't have time for it. I guess I'd been hoping she would realize how scary the situation was to my husband and me. Whatever the reason for her lousy bedside manner, it didn't make me feel secure.

As she walked to the sink to wash her hands, she said, "So what are we taking a look at today?"

"The area I talked to you about a couple of months ago—I've noticed that it has started to grow. It's very tender now."

While she examined me, she asked, "Do you have a history of breast cancer in your family?"

"No, ma'am. No one in my family has ever had cancer."

After examining me, she sat in her rolling chair and said, "You most likely have nothing to be worried about. As I said before, it's probably a cyst. You should watch your caffeine intake."

"Would it be possible to get a mammogram, so we can make sure it's not something to be concerned about?" Steve requested.

With an annoyed sigh, she said, "Because you're so young, insurance won't cover the cost of a mammogram unless you have a doctor's referral."

"Could you please give me a referral?" I asked hesitantly.

She pulled the script pad from her pocket and began to scribble something on the paper.

As she handed me the referral she said, "Hopefully this will give you the peace of mind you're looking for."

I managed a half smile and mumbled "thank you" as she left.

I took the gown off and started putting my clothes back on. I felt conflicted, torn between wanting to be reassured by her confidence, yet a bit embarrassed and even belittled by her insistence that it was no big deal. I had always been told that you must be your own health advocate. I knew what I felt. And I wasn't a hypochondriac. Why was she so insensitive to my concern? Should I even pursue this? After all, she was so convinced I had no need to be worried.

Steve was sweet. "Babe, don't listen to her," he said. "We'll get the mammogram and see what's going on."

After I finished dressing, the emotion of the situation caught up with me and I began to cry. Steve hugged me and said, "It'll be okay."

Hand in hand, we left the examining room.

Because she had been so insistent that what I felt was nothing to be concerned about—and, I admit it, because I was afraid—I waited a couple more weeks before I made the appointment for a mammogram.

The day finally came for my mammogram appointment—a beautiful spring morning in late May of 2003. I told Steve he didn't need to come because I was sure it was nothing.

Walking into the breast-imaging center and approaching the reception desk, I felt calmed by the soft lighting and the fragrance of pink roses. The receptionist greeted me with a warm smile, handed me a clipboard, and asked me to fill out the forms and bring them back when I was finished. On my way to an open seat I noticed that I was the youngest woman waiting to be seen. For some reason that made me feel very uncomfortable. *What are you doing here, Sarah?* I thought. *This is so silly. You're just overreacting. Why are you making such a big deal out of this?*

A short, blonde woman in pink scrubs, wearing bright pink lipstick, came out to the lobby and called out, "Sarah McLean."

I stood, smiled, and followed her to the dressing room where she handed me the gown and said kindly, "Once you're dressed, just have a seat in the waiting area. I'll be back to get you shortly."

The waiting area was so nice, decorated with just the right amount of feminine décor, that I felt welcome and taken care of. An antique buffet served as a small coffee bar. The seats were cozy and inviting, and a selection of ladies' magazines lay nearby.

I sat next to a woman who looked twice my age. Nervously, I grabbed a magazine. As I waited, with my eyes locked on the magazine so I didn't have to make eye contact with any of the ladies, my head was filled with thoughts: *Is this going to hurt? How are they going to do a mammogram when my boobs are so small? These ladies probably think I'm crazy.*

After ten minutes, the kind technician returned and said, "Sarah, right this way."

We walked into a dark room with a big mammography machine. A technician waiting next

---

This can't be happening to me. I'm only twenty-six years old. I've only been married for a year. I haven't had children yet.

---

to the machine said, "Please take off the gown and step up to the machine."

I stepped up to the device. She raised my right arm above my head and firmly pressed my chest into the machine, saying, "Please forgive me if my hands are cold. You will feel some pressure as we get your breast in the right position. I know it's uncomfortable smashing your breast like a pancake, but bear with me. I'll get it done as quickly as possible."

I laughed. "I'm okay. Thanks for being so compassionate and understanding." Her kindness and sense of humor put me at ease. I appreciated her effort to make me comfortable in such an uncomfortable situation.

She took several pictures from different angles. I stood there looking at the ceiling, my stomach filled with butterflies, wondering what the outcome would be.

Eventually she said, "Go ahead and put the gown back on. I'll be back in a moment to take you to the radiologist's office."

After I'd pulled the gown back on, I paused for a moment to catch my breath. I put my hands on the side of the bed, leaned over it, and hung my head. Eyes closed, I considered the possible outcomes. I was so scared. *Here we go. Here's the moment of truth. What will he say? I'm sure the doctor is going to come in and reassure me there's nothing to be concerned with, right?*

The technician opened the door and said, "Come with me." She led me to an examining room a couple doors down. "Wait here and the doctor will be with you in a moment. He has to review the films."

After what felt like an eternity, there was a knock on the door.

"Hi, Sarah. How are you today?" the doctor said as he reached to shake my hand. The nurse followed him into the room. He put the mammography films on the screen for me to look at and said, "I've reviewed your films, and there was a spot that looked concerning to me."

What was he saying? My heart began beating way too fast; I could feel it in my ears. My palms got sweaty. The nurse began to rub my back as the doctor said something about wanting to do a biopsy.

"Because of your age I'd like to get you in as soon as possible, so we can see what we're dealing with," he said with concern as he leaned forward, looking intently into my eyes.

I didn't know what to think. My mind was on overload. My mouth began to move, but I wasn't sure what I was saying. It felt as if everything was spinning, fuzzy—like I was in a dream.

"Okay," I said. That was all I could get out.

The nurse told me, "We'll make the appointment for you at the front desk."

It was surreal. I couldn't believe what I was hearing. It was like an out-of-body experience. My thoughts raced. *This can't really be happening to me. I'm only twenty-six years old. I've only been married for a year. I haven't had children yet. This isn't the kind of thing I'm supposed to have to think about. This is something my mom, aunt, or grandmother would be facing—not me.*

They scheduled the biopsy for the following day.

I walked out to my car and climbed in. I closed my eyes and felt the heat of the sun beating on my face. I didn't know what to do. I felt numb. I couldn't even cry. My hands were shaking. After a few minutes, I rummaged through my purse and found my phone. Trying to keep my hands steady, I dialed Steve's number.

He answered after one ring, his voice anxious.

"Babe," I said, "the doctor found some calcification in the mammogram and he wants to do a biopsy tomorrow."

"What did he say exactly?" Steve asked.

"I'm not sure. He's just concerned about the spot, so he wants to biopsy it and see if it's anything."

We just sat in silence. I knew he wanted answers. So did I. But there were no answers to give. Until we did the biopsy, we wouldn't know exactly what we were dealing with. I could sense that he felt as helpless as I did. *Could this really be cancer? What were we going to do?*

The next morning, both Steve and my mom went with me for the biopsy. As the three of us sat filling the air with nervous chatter in the waiting room, I tried to put on a happy face, but inside my stomach was all in knots. I tried to stay engaged in the conversation, but I could only focus on what was about to happen. I was so scared.

Eventually I was led to the procedure room. Holding my gown closed, I felt a chill in the air. The room was very bright; windows all around the perimeter flooded the room with sunshine. In the middle of the room was a big metal table with a hole where my breasts would go.

Several nurses were already in the room, preparing for the biopsy. Everyone was so friendly and kind. We casually talked about the day's events as I waited for them to tell me what to do next. They were trying their best to keep things casual and get my mind off things, but I felt like I was going to throw up.

"Please remove your gown and get up on the table face down," one of the nurses said. "Place your breasts in the opening, so the doctor can reach you."

As I climbed up on the cold metal table, I began to shake a little—not only from the chill in the air, but also from fear. I took a couple of deep breaths to calm myself. The nurse covered me with warm blankets.

The doctor came in. He asked how I was feeling, then said, "Let's get started. I'm going to raise the table, so I can position you where I can insert the needle and take a sample of the tissue. Please stay very still."

With my face down in a crescent-shaped pillow, like the type used during a massage, I answered as calmly as I could. "Okay."

He said, "You're going to feel a stick. That's the local anesthetic we're using to numb the breast."

With my teeth gritted and fists clenched in anticipation, I uneasily said, "All right."

When I was numb, he made a small incision and used a needle to extract a sample of the tissue from the lump inside my breast. I was awake the entire time, listening to him talk with the nurses. I continued to lie still, but my mind was running wild. A small tear rolled down my face as I pondered the possibilities. *What will I do if this is cancer? Will I lose my hair? Will I lose my breast? Will I be able to have children? Will I die? Can I do this?*

The procedure lasted about an hour. When he finished, the doctor said, "You did a great job. I'll send this tissue sample over to the pathology lab. They should have the results within the next couple of days." *The next couple of days?* I thought. *I want to know now. Why does this process take so long?*

"Okay. Thank you." I didn't know what else to say.

I went home that afternoon. As the anesthetic wore off, the biopsy area was pretty tender, so I just took it easy and anxiously awaited the phone call with the results.

The next morning I still didn't feel great, so I decided to stay home and rest. Steve was at work. I curled up on the couch with a warm blanket and my Pomeranian, Pete, waiting for the call. It's crazy how your mind can go wild when you're faced with a situation you can't control. I felt like a hamster running feverishly on a wheel but getting nowhere.

At around 3:00 in the afternoon, the phone rang, startling me out of the daze I had put myself into with my endless, fearful speculation.

I took a deep breath and answered the phone. "Sarah, this is Dr. Evans." Dr. Evans was my primary care physician. Her name was on file to be contacted with any results. "I received a call from the pathology lab today. They advised me you had a breast biopsy yesterday. They gave me the results."

There was a long pause. Then she continued: "I'm so sorry to have to tell you this. The biopsy was positive. You have cancer."

Chapter Two
Will I Look Deformed?

I couldn't believe my ears. Surely this was a mistake. These were supposed to be the best days of my life. How could I be going through something like this?

Dr. Evans went on to say, "I've contacted a breast surgeon for you and made an appointment for next week. Ready to write down his number?"

Still in shock, I couldn't connect with the meaning of her words. It didn't seem real. "Hold on a minute," I said. "Let me get something to write with."

I grabbed for a pen and paper. When I finished taking down all the information, she said, "I'm so sorry, sweetheart. Please let us know if there is anything we can do. I will check on you in a couple of days."

I hung up the phone and then sat there staring at the wall. I tucked my knees up into my chest and wrapped my arms around them in a fetal position. My eyes welled up with tears, and soon I was weeping. I felt so alone. A rush of thoughts flooded my mind.

How could this be happening? I don't understand. I'm healthy. I'm too young. Will I be able to have babies? Am I going to die?

After I regained my composure, I called Steve.

"Honey, I just got a call from the doctor."

"Did they get the results?" he asked nervously.

Trying to hold back the tears I said, "Yes, it's positive. I have cancer."

We sat silently at either end of the phone. Neither of us knew what to say.

Finally, Steve lovingly said, "I know you're scared, but I love you and we're going to get through this."

Steve was an amazing support to me—so strong even in the midst of such weakness. My heart was crumbling, but he was there to hold me up. And I realized even at the time how fortunate I was. There are so many women out there—perhaps you—who don't have this type of support system when they get their diagnosis. Hearing those words, "You have cancer," is a shocking and lonely feeling. It's so hard to go through it alone. That's why it's wonderful that, even for those who have no supportive husband or family support system, there is a sisterhood of survivors longing to love us through our journey. We'll talk later in the book about how to connect with that system, if you haven't already.

"I love you too," I said.

❀ ❀ ❀

Everything progressed quickly. It was as if I were caught in a tornado. Those who've been through a cancer diagnosis—or for that matter, any number of other major life disruptions—can identify with that, I'm sure. Your life can feel like a tornado, full of unexpected ups and downs and twists and turns. We feel as if we're being thrown all over the place. Tornados arrive quickly, seemingly out of nowhere, and leave a path of destruction in their wake.

I had no idea what was to come, and I was terrified.

The next week, I went for a consultation with my breast surgeon, Dr. Marinelli. Steve and my mom sat with me in the examination room, waiting for the doctor. Waiting—I seemed to be doing a lot of that. Scared as I was, I was still eager to get the ball rolling. Once I'd heard what he had to say, I would have a better idea what this journey would look like. The "not knowing" was driving me crazy, especially since the whole process was subject to everyone else's timeline and not just my own. I wanted answers! I wanted to know what to expect. But I had to wait for appointments. This was my cancer, and I thought we should be expediting everything. But for everyone else, this was their day-to-day business. I had to realize and accept that I wasn't their only patient. They were moving as fast as they could. I would have to be patient.

There was a knock at the door, and a short, smiling older man with snow-white hair entered with a jovial "Good morning."

Over the next hour, we sat and talked about the process of a lumpectomy surgery. Dr. Marinelli explained that he would give me his recommendation, but whatever decision there was to be made was mine.

Because of the stage and type of cancer I had, he recommended that I have a lumpectomy followed by radiation. Not every breast cancer patient hears that recommendation from their doctor, since our individual treatment plans are dependent on factors that vary from case to case.

"I'll remove a quarter of your breast," Dr. Marinelli said. "After I've removed the tumor, I'll biopsy the surrounding tissue to verify we have clear margins—meaning that we got all the cancerous cells."

I barely have any boobs to begin with. How deformed would this look?

He was so kind and comforting that I trusted him and his judgment from the beginning. His warm presence and genuine concern put my heart at ease because I knew I was in good hands. As we ended the consultation he asked, "Do you have any questions?" I said, "No, I think you've explained everything." I glanced at Steve and my mom to see if they had any questions. For all three of us, this was one of those moments when you don't know what you don't know, so we had no clue what to ask.

The truth is, despite the good information I was given by doctors, I had no clue what I was walking into. I asked no questions that morning because I had no idea what questions to ask. And I had no friends who were survivors—friends who'd been through it, who could coach me.

Am I going to look deformed? Will my clothes fit right? How will Steve look at me?

Sitting in Dr. Marinelli's office, Steve and I talked it over and decided the lumpectomy was the best option for me. We scheduled the surgery for the following week. I knew this surgery would change my physical appearance by removing a quarter of my right breast. During the week before surgery I wondered what I would look like and whether I would be able to accept my new body—changed forever. *Am I going to look deformed? Will my clothes fit right? How will Steve look at me?* I prayed a lot, asking God to give me the strength to accept and embrace the new me.

On the day of surgery, we arrived at the hospital early in the morning. The nurse started an IV, and I sat anxiously waiting to be taken back to the operating room.

Several family members, friends, and pastors joined Steve and me in the pre-op room to pray. As the pastor prayed, I felt a warm presence wash over me. I felt confident that everything was going to be all right. The overwhelming support from family and friends was so humbling. Seeing the expressions of love on their faces enabled me to discern God's love in a new and profound way. God was showing his love for me through these amazing people who had rallied around me. If they could love me this much, then how much could my heavenly Father love me? Shortly after we prayed, the nurses came in and said, "It's time to go. Give your hugs and kisses."

Steve leaned in to kiss me and whispered, "I love you."

As our cheeks touched, I could feel the tears rolling gently down his face. I looked tenderly at him and wiped away his tear. "I love you too."

The nurses slowly rolled the bed down the long, narrow hallway; green and white tiles lined the halls. It made me think of a prison hospital from the 1970s. The smell of iodine filled the air. I felt like a prisoner being taken to her cell.

When we pushed through the double doors of the bright, icy-cold operating room, several nurses were already there, awaiting my arrival. It felt so good when the nurses draped cozy, warm blankets over me. The anesthesiologist came in, but all I remember is him asking me a series of questions and I drifted off to sleep.

✿ ✿ ✿

After the surgery, Dr. Marinelli came out to the waiting area and gave Steve an update. He explained that he had removed the tumor and biopsied the surrounding tissue. He strongly believed the breast cavity still contained cancer, but he wouldn't know for sure until he received the pathology report. He told Steve he would call within the next couple of days to give me the results. Steve didn't know what to think. Was he going to lose his wife? He felt so helpless—there was nothing he could do to protect me or improve my situation. He passed along the doctor's report to our family and friends.

After I woke up in post-op, I still had to wait there for an hour before I could go home. Steve helped me get dressed, and we headed home to wait for the results. As we drove home, I wondered what was beneath the bandages. Would I look deformed? Would I still be as pretty to Steve as I was before? Would I still feel as feminine, having such an intimate part of my body taken from me? Would I think I was beautiful or be repulsed by my own body?

Once we got home and settled, my dad made my favorite dinner for me. He was a great cook, and that was his way of caring for me. Steve was right by my side to help me any way he could.

I fell asleep for a while as the anesthesia wore off. When I woke up, Steve hesitantly explained what Dr. Marinelli had told him after the surgery—that he wasn't confident he'd gotten it all, and we should hear something within the next couple of days.

My heart was heavy. I thought the hard part was behind us!

> It was as if I were saying good-bye to the
> image in the mirror. I knew I would wake
> up the next day with an entirely different
> body. I studied everything about myself,
> from my hair to my eyes to my breasts.

The next morning Dr. Marinelli called. After our greetings, he paused for a moment and then said, "Sarah, I've gotten the pathology results from the biopsy. I'm so sorry to tell you this, but the cancer has already spread throughout the entire right breast. Because you're so young, I want to recommend a radical bilateral mastectomy."

I thought, *I don't even really know what a radical bilateral mastectomy is.* I knew that mastectomy meant removal of the breast, but I didn't know what "radical bilateral" meant. Soon, I would find out: A radical bilateral mastectomy is a more invasive surgery compared to a traditional bilateral mastectomy. In a radical bilateral mastectomy, the surgeon removes all the tissue from the collarbone through the entire breast area on the left and right sides, including the lymph nodes under the armpits; most of the time, nipples are removed as well, but some women have the option to preserve their nipples, depending on the type of breast cancer.

I heard myself saying through tears, "Okay. When do you want to do this?"

"Before we do the mastectomy, you'll need to meet with my partner, who is a plastic surgeon," he said compassionately. "We want to see if you're a candidate for immediate reconstruction."

He reassured me that he was confident he could get all the infected tissue with this more radical surgery, so that I wouldn't have to go through extensive therapy like chemo or radiation. I felt wary of his confidence, especially since the first doctor had been so confident that my lump "was nothing." She had been dead wrong.

I hung up the phone, once again not knowing what to think or how to feel. Déjà vu. I just sat on my couch staring at the wall, feeling numb with disbelief. It was as if I were watching a movie of someone else's life. *What in the world was going on? God, where are you?*

A few days later, Steve and I sat in the office of Dr. Shah, the plastic surgeon—a short, older gentleman from India. As he entered the room, his soft voice brought me a refreshing sense of comfort. But this was a landmark day for me, and not an easy one. In order to examine me, Dr. Shah would have to remove the bandages. This would be the first time I had seen myself since the lumpectomy.

As he removed the bandages, I looked down. The difference was evident—my right breast was drastically smaller than the left—and I hadn't had much there to begin with.

He peered over the top of his glasses as he examined me. I wondered: Would he be able to fix the uneven appearance?

I quickly discovered he was a man of few words. With his thick Indian accent, he explained the reconstruction options to us. It's amazing what plastic surgeons are able to do with breast reconstruction. I had no idea.

We discussed whether I was a candidate for flap reconstruction or implant reconstruction. A flap reconstruction is where the doctor takes healthy tissue from another part of your body and transplants it to the breast. The other option was tissue expanders, where a balloon is implanted in your chest to stretch the skin. Once the skin is stretched, you go in for another surgery and have the tissue expander removed and the implant inserted.

By the end of the meeting Steve and I agreed with Dr. Shah that, because of my size and age, immediate reconstruction with tissue expanders followed by implants would be the best choice for me. We left the office that day with the surgery on the books for June 5, 2003.

In the days leading up to the surgery, my mind was consumed by fear. At work, I could feel the sympathetic stares of my coworkers. As we passed in the hallway, they would give me a supportive smile. While I appreciated their compassion and concern, I was painfully aware of how I stood out. No other employees at the church had ever been diagnosed with cancer. I could tell they felt sorry for me, but they didn't know what to say. Honestly, I wouldn't have known what to say to someone either.

The day finally arrived. I hadn't slept a wink the night before. My mind wouldn't slow down for me to rest. Thankfully, I didn't have to be at the hospital until noon, so I took my time getting ready.

With the bathroom door closed, I stood in front of the mirror brushing my teeth, trying to understand the magnitude of what was about to happen.

It was as if I were saying good-bye to the image in the mirror. I knew I would wake up the next day with an entirely different body. I studied everything about myself, from my hair to my eyes to my breasts.

I gazed deep into the eyes of the woman staring back at me. Tears welled, and as I hung my head, they started to flow. I knew this surgery was something I needed so I could be healthy and live a long life, but I didn't want to go through the pain. I didn't want to be a burden to my family. I didn't want my life to change. My heart was breaking. *Would I know this new woman tomorrow? Could I embrace her? Could Steve embrace her?*

As we walked cautiously into the hospital, I knew my life was about to change forever. Once I'd filled out the paperwork, a nurse guided me to a room for a pre-op procedure. As I lay on the table, still in my street clothes except she'd had me remove everything above the waist, she inserted four needles through my right nipple to inject a dye that would locate any lymph nodes that needed to be removed once we were in surgery. This was done without anesthetic, so I held my breath because the pain was more than I could bear. Eyes tightly shut, I grimaced each time she injected another needle.

This world of cancer was so foreign. I'm a detail person—I like to know every single thing that will happen, but I was clueless to all the steps—like this painful injection.

Once the injections were finished, the nurse escorted me to a different part of the hospital, where they had me put on the hospital gown for the operation. The nurse started my IV. After all the preparations had been completed, the nurse brought Steve into the room to give me one last kiss before they wheeled me back. He leaned in, brushed my hair with his hand and whispered, "I love you, Babe. You're the strongest person I know."

With an overwhelming sense of terror and anxiety, I looked into his eyes and said "Thank you, Honey. I love you too."

He left the room. The nurses asked, "Are you ready?"

Fearful but determined, I said, "I'm as ready as I'll ever be. Let's do this."

As they wheeled my gurney to the operating room, one of the nurses held my hand and said, "You're in great hands. Don't worry. We'll take wonderful care of you."

Those simple words were exactly what I needed to hear at that moment. I took a few deep breaths to try to release the anxiety gripping me.

My anesthesiologist, Dr. Molina, an older man with a thick Peruvian accent, came into the operating room. His commanding presence earned respect and attention from everyone in the room. In his heavily accented English, he told me to start counting down from 100. With the oxygen mask covering my face, I started counting down: "100, 99, 98, 97…" My eyes were getting heavy. Off to sleep I went.

My first memory, five hours later, was of waking briefly and looking at Steve by my bedside. I quickly fell back asleep. When I awoke again, my body was in such horrific pain that I remember moaning because it was so bad. I had a morphine pump that allowed me to administer morphine but only at regulated intervals. Steve called the nurse to see if there was anything else we could do for the pain.

The next thing I remember was waking up the next morning in ICU. I was still heavily medicated, so I was very groggy. I kept asking Steve, "What's going on? Why am I in ICU? I don't understand."

He didn't answer—as if he was afraid to tell me. The nurse asked him, "Can you please step out for a minute, so I can check her vitals?"

Once he'd left the room, I asked the nurse, "Why am I here?"

She said, "You overdosed on morphine last night and stopped breathing."

Oh, my God. I almost died. Fear crept over me like a blanket. My heart raced. As she wrapped the blood pressure cuff around my arm, the nurse continued. "You were brought to ICU and given Narcan. That's a drug that reverses the effects of all the other drugs in your body, so we could get you regulated."

"Why did that happen?" I asked.

"You didn't have any more morphine than you were supposed to, but your heart got so relaxed that you fell asleep and stopped breathing."

"Am I okay now?" I asked.

"Yes, we've gotten you stabilized. You'll be just fine," she said, and left.

I lay there alone for a few minutes before Steve came back into the room. I didn't know what was worse—the excruciating pain I was feeling, or the news the nurse had just given me. I was so scared. *How had this happened? And would it happen again? If the morphine had caused it, was it safe for me to continue to use it? And if I couldn't, how could I hope to manage this pain?* It was almost too much to bear.

When Steve came back in, I asked, "Why didn't you tell me what happened?"

"Because I didn't want to scare you any more than you already were."

"Tell me what happened. Were you there the whole time?"

"Well, they brought you to your room around 7:00 p.m.," he said. "You were still asleep from the anesthesia. But you looked … strange. Your skin was very pale. I held your hand and watched you sleep. Around nine o'clock, you started waking up." He lowered his head down and paused for a moment. Then he looked up again and continued, his eyes filled with tears.

"You opened your eyes for a moment and smiled at me. I told you I loved you. Then you adjusted your head on the pillow to find a more comfortable position, closed your eyes, and drifted back to sleep. The TV was on—I was watching the ESPN highlights, but still holding your hand, and I noticed it felt a little cold. After a couple minutes, I looked back at you." Gradually, his emotions had been getting closer to the surface—by now his nose was running and his face was red and splotchy; tears ran down his cheeks.

"Something was wrong. Like *terribly* wrong. I pressed the button over and over to call the nurses' station, then I raced to the door to see if anyone was coming. But as soon as I opened the door, an army of nurses and doctors barreled in. I've never been so scared. I just tried to stay out of the way—I watched from over in the corner. It was mass chaos! The medical team unhooked your bed and rushed you out into the hallway and away. It only took an instant, and you were gone and I was alone in the room. Someone had said they were taking you to ICU. I was leaning back against the wall, and I collapsed into a fetal position and sobbed. I felt like my heart was being ripped out of my chest. Thoughts flooded my mind. What would I do if I lost you? How could I go on?" He paused, looking deep into me. "You are my world," he said.

After a moment, he went on. "A nurse came back and escorted me to the ICU waiting room. Several hours went by. As I paced the floor, I could hear you screaming—I guess from the pain. I felt numb. It was like I was in a dream. Why was this happening to you and not me? I felt so guilty and helpless— like there was something I should do to make this go away, but there was nothing I could do.

"Finally a doctor came in and called my name. He said, 'We've revived her. She's awake now.' I asked him if you were going to be okay, and he said, 'Sarah will be just fine.' He told me what happened and reassured me everything was all right."

He put his head against mine and held my hand. We cried together. Steve was as scared as I was.

I stayed in the hospital four days. Because of the near-death incident, the doctors wanted to keep a close watch on me and make sure everything was okay before they released me to go home.

While we were in the hospital, Dr. Marinelli came to check on me every day. On the second day, he told us the pathology report had come back clear. He was able to get all the cancerous cells with surgery. That meant I wouldn't have to undergo radiation or chemotherapy. Praise God! At last—a piece of good news! That was just what I'd needed to hear.

Finally it was time to go home. Dr. Marinelli said, "My patients do much better when they're in their own environment," and I knew just what he meant. I was more than ready to be in my own bed. Once I came home, I'm sure I began to heal much faster. But the surgeries were only the beginning of a long and painful reconstruction process.

After the surgery Dr. Marinelli had put a tight compression vest on me to keep the swelling down. For the four days I was in the hospital, I wasn't able to look at myself—I was too scared to look beneath the veil. Magical thinking, I guess—if I didn't look at it, it wasn't true. But after I'd been home about five days, Steve helped me into the bathtub one morning. I wasn't able to get my chest submerged in water yet—the compression vest was still on—but I wanted to soak my legs.

Eyes closed, I took a deep breath and enjoyed the warmth of the water flowing from the faucet. Steve squeezed some cucumber-melon body wash onto a washcloth and softly washed my face, my neck, behind my ears, and the rest of my body. The water felt so refreshing and the gentle touch of the cloth was so relaxing. It had been five days since I'd had a shower, so I sat in the tub soaking in the warm water, enjoying the moment. How grateful I was to have such a loving husband who was willing to help me.

I was so humbled. I had never had to rely solely on anyone else; not being able to do the day-to-day

things for myself, even things like brushing my hair
or wiping my butt, was an agonizing situation for me.
I considered myself to be an independent woman,
and I had always prided myself on being able to take
care of myself. I derived strength from knowing I
was responsible, dependable, and capable of doing
things on my own. I didn't *need* anyone to help me.
But at least for now, that was no longer true, and it
was teaching me humility.

After Steve finished bathing me, he helped me
out of the tub and patted me dry. We stood there
face to face, and I quietly said, "Babe, can I have a
minute alone?"

He knew from the look in my eyes that I was
finally ready to discover the new body that lay
beneath the vest. "Are you sure?"

I sighed and said, "Yes, … I think so."

He stepped out of the bathroom and slowly
closed the door.

I quietly locked it behind him. I didn't want
anyone walking in. *What if they saw how horrible I
looked?*

I stood staring into the eyes of the girl in the
mirror one last time before unzipping the vest.
Slowly, I reached for the zipper and began to pull it
down. When I finished unzipping the vest I paused
for a moment before I could muster the courage to
pull it open.

Gradually I pulled back the left side, then the
right. Underneath the vest were mounds of bandages
to soak up the oozing blood. I removed the bandages

gently. What I saw underneath shocked me. Two lines. That was it. No nipples. No breasts.

I hung my head, shamed. My eyes filled with tears and a deep river of pain and sorrow washed through me and overflowed through my eyes. The depth and power of my grief was like someone who had just lost a dear loved one.

I felt like a monster. I hated what I saw. I looked like a little boy. Even though I knew the surgery had been necessary to save my life, I began doubting myself. But no amount of doubt or second-guessing would change anything. There was no going back. For the first time, I felt the gravity of the decision I had made. My life had been forever changed.

A flood of lies invaded my mind. *You're repulsive. How can your husband love you now? You're not a woman anymore. You're so ugly. You look deformed. How will you ever feel feminine again? You'll never again be beautiful.*

What have I done?

Chapter Three
Who Is Sarah Now?

In a state of shock, I zipped the vest back up, wiped my face, and opened the bathroom door. Those few minutes had been as long as I could bear to look at the horror my chest had become.

Steve was waiting in the living room. "Are you okay?" he asked.

I couldn't speak. I fell into his arms and began to sob. He wrapped his arms around me, giving me the space to weep. The comfort of his touch was exactly what I needed in that moment, giving me a mental picture of how God holds us when we're hurting. His embrace was a reflection of God's love for his daughters.

It felt as if my identity had been stolen. Now that I had seen beneath the bandages, I didn't know who I was anymore. *Who was Sarah now?* I had thought I'd known. Now I wasn't sure.

I was beginning a journey that would teach me much. Sometimes in life, we don't really know who we are—or more importantly *whose* we are—until we go through trials that strip our souls bare and reveal our true self. This would be that kind of trial.

I would also learn much on this journey about the true nature of beauty. What I had just seen in the mirror, I thought as Steve comforted me and I continued to weep, didn't fit the description of beauty. And maybe it didn't, if you accept the world's definition of beauty, as so many women do in these times. But beauty as our society defines it is a false sense of beauty. We're inundated with misleading images in magazines, movies, and TV shows that try to reinforce that false definition of beauty and self-worth. So many women are dying in a sea of self-hatred and inadequacy because we're wrapped up in the lie that unless we attain a certain appearance, we aren't truly beautiful.

✿ ✿ ✿

I spent the next four weeks on medical leave. Every other week, I would visit the plastic surgeon, Dr. Shah. He would insert a needle into the port of the tissue expander in my chest and inject saline into the expander. I dreaded these visits. I didn't have a lot of excess skin, so the injections were exceptionally painful. And since I didn't have a lot of elasticity in my skin, it was a very slow process. This process not only stretched my skin, it also stretched my chest and back muscles because the tissue expander had been placed behind the breast muscle during surgery. As the apparatus expanded, it stretched the muscle and

Sometimes in life, we don't really know who we are—or more importantly *whose* we are—until we go through trials that strip our souls bare and reveal our true self. This would be that kind of trial.

thus created a pocket of skin to accommodate an implant. It was very time-consuming. For me, it took about six months for my skin to stretch enough to accommodate an implant.

After four weeks, I went back to work. All my coworkers were so concerned and supportive. When I walked down the hall people would smile and ask how I was doing. I would smile politely and say, "I'm doing all right. Just taking it one step at a time." What a world of insecurity hid behind those mild, misleading words. I felt every stare, heard every whisper. I knew that people weren't talking bad about me, but I felt different—different from who I had been before, and different from the rest of the people in the office. I was going through a major life-changing experience that no one else I knew had gone through. I had no one to lean on for comfort and guidance, no one who had been here before me. And the physical transformation, difficult and painful as it was, was just the beginning. God was about to take me through a spiritual transformation that would forever change me on the inside.

✿ ✿ ✿

For much of my life, I had been obsessed with what other people thought of me. My identity had been wrapped up in the approval of others. I understood intellectually that I was a child of God, created in his image, but my heart lacked the confidence and security that knowledge should have given me. When you're made in the image of God, should it matter what others think of you?

Logically, I knew the cancer had been removed, so I should have been able to move on with my life, right? It wasn't that easy for me.

Just the opposite. Even though I was surrounded by people who loved me and were willing to do anything to help me, I felt more alone than I had ever felt in my life. I felt so isolated. I didn't feel like I could relate with anyone because the core of who I am was being challenged on every level. My physical body had been transformed, and I didn't know what shape my heart would be in by the time I had adjusted to the new reality of my life.

Despair is a good word for the emotional place I was in. But in that despair, God was beginning to soften my heart to his promises and open my eyes to the way he sees me. His promise in Psalm 139:14 tells us: "I praise you because I am fearfully and wonderfully made; your works are wonderful, I know that full well."

How could I go on with a "business as usual" mentality after facing my own mortality? I had been operated on for a type of cancer that kills many women each year. And I had nearly died from a reaction to the anesthetic. Those things changed me. Life would never be the same.

Unfortunately, I didn't know any other survivors—especially survivors my age. I looked online and called around to find a support group that catered to young survivors, but found nothing, and eventually I gave up searching. And yet, surrounded by people who hadn't experienced what I had, I thought I stuck out like a sore thumb. I didn't really know what to talk about in conversations anymore. I knew that people wanted to ask me questions, but they didn't know how. And some just ignored the situation because talking about it made them uncomfortable. *Was I just being too sensitive when I felt that others saw me as different?* As "the twenty-six-year-old girl who had cancer and had her boobs cut off"? Steve, my family, and friends were more than willing to discuss it all with me, or to just let me talk, but even so, it seemed impossible to explain my emotional ups and downs to someone who had never traveled this road. Even if that "someone" is someone you love. No amount of words is enough to get the job done.

An array of emotions stirred inside me. My mind felt like a top spinning out of control, filled with so many thoughts I didn't know how to process them. On one hand, I felt I needed to be strong, positive, to press on, and not be overly emotional. On the other hand I felt weak, scared, angry, and sad. It was an enormously lonely feeling.

In those moments of isolation, we're vulnerable to being pulled into a place of darkness. Isolated, lonely, lacking the perspective of others—that's when the lies and deceptions that the enemy of God, Satan, speaks to our hearts can take root, drawing us deeper and deeper into hopelessness.

Until I knew where the lies, misunderstandings, and false perceptions that were tripping me up had come from, I couldn't overcome them so that I could surrender myself to God's will. Unfortunately, the process of exploring our history can be grueling and laborious. Even so, the pain of self-discovery is worth it if it gives us the capacity to transcend our past and embrace our future.

So where had all these lies, misunderstandings, and false perceptions come from?

Chapter Four
The Flawless Façade

Steve and I married on September 1, 2001. Exactly a year later, on September 1, 2002, we moved from Dallas, Texas, to Oklahoma City, Oklahoma.

For a year before we decided to move to Oklahoma, we had prayed fervently about our future and God's direction for our family. Despite my fears and reservations, we both had a deep longing to discover God's will for our lives. In our hearts, we had an unexplainable sense of destiny and calling, but it wasn't a clear picture—more like a fog. We could only see right in front of us, but we knew that, beyond that thick cloud of the unknown, there was something great.

During our times of prayer and conversation, we felt led toward Oklahoma City. My family lived in Oklahoma City, and Steve had a lot of close family and friends from college who lived there too. The potential for a bigger, closer community of friends and family was tempting. It would be a wonderful place to raise a family someday.

This was a life-changing decision, and despite the advantages we saw in Oklahoma City, I stayed on the fence about it for several months. Steve patiently waited for me to warm up to the idea. Morning after morning, on my ride to work, I would talk to God as I sat in Dallas traffic, asking, *What is your will for us, God? Do you want us to move to Oklahoma? What if it's not the right decision? Will you still love us if we mess up? What will I do for work?* I was so afraid of making the wrong decision that I was paralyzed.

And that was not a new phenomenon for me.

✿ ✿ ✿

I had always believed in God. From my earliest memories, my parents had practically raised me in church. But since becoming an adult, I had discovered that I didn't truly trust God in the depths of my soul, nor did I understand his grace.

I'm far from the only person who has ever felt this way, but I had formed an image of God as a harsh, authoritarian being somewhere far removed from my daily life, just waiting to strike me down the moment I made a mistake. At least, that's how I unconsciously related to him. I had head knowledge of him from all those years in church, but what I didn't have was a relationship with him that came from my heart. And oh, I wanted that intimate understanding of God—more than anything. More than anything, that is, except control of my own life.

Deep down, I knew that God had a plan and a purpose for my life, but I was afraid to let him reveal it to me. If I'd truly believed he had good things in store for me, perhaps I would have surrendered to him—but, crippled by fear, I was squelching the voice of God relentlessly pursuing my heart. After all, what if something went wrong? What if he didn't come through for me? What if this process of letting go proved to be too painful? What if I didn't like what he had planned for me? What if I couldn't complete the task he had for me? What if I failed?

This crisis over our decision to move or not was typical of my deep fears and anxieties that came from wrong thinking and false perceptions of God. For so long, I believed I wasn't good enough in his eyes (or anyone else's), that I was a failure—so to me, it was crucial that I didn't make the wrong decision about the move. I didn't want God to be mad at me or disappointed with me.

❖ ❖ ❖

After many agonizing months, we finally decided: We would take a leap of faith. Once we'd made the decision, after the months of uncertainty, I felt a bit torn: a calming sense that this was the right decision on one hand and continuing uncertainty on the other. But I would never know what my future held unless I faced my fear, stepped out in faith, and risked walking into the unknown.

Steve and I were very young, our marriage was also very young, and we were ready for this new adventure together! Once I got used to the idea of moving, we were both eager to see what God had in store for us in Oklahoma City.

When we first arrived, Steve began a transitional job at a car dealership, and I was pursuing work at the State Bureau of Investigation because of my work background, but God had different plans.

We had started going to church with my sister. One Sunday morning after we'd been in Oklahoma City just a few weeks, I sat down before the service started and examined the bulletin. There was a position posted for an executive assistant. I thought, *I could do that.* The next morning I faxed my résumé. A couple days later the church called me for an interview; I was hired by the end of the week.

Despite all my uncertainty earlier, now I felt a confident assurance that I was in God's will, exactly where I was supposed to be for this season of my life. My heart was filled with a mysterious peace that couldn't be explained with words.

Working at the church was like entering a foreign country; the surroundings were different, the language was different, the culture was different. Before this job, I had always worked in a corporate environment: stuffy, sterile, and with everything done by the rule book. I had never before worked in a place where people were passionate about their relationship with God or where you were allowed to pray together, worship together, and take time out for Bible study. Was this place real? Who gets to go to a place like this for work every day?

I had no idea this was the beginning of my spiritual awakening. Working at the church ignited in me a ravishing hunger for the Word of God. Even though I had gone to church most of my life, only now did I realize how much I really didn't *know* God. I only knew about him, so I dove into learning more about God's character.

And God showed me that I didn't accurately understand his heart. The more I read, meditated, and reflected on his promises, the more my heart was propelled into a metamorphosis—and like any metamorphosis, this one would be accompanied by a change in behavior, a change in environment, and growing pains. I would never have been able to predict which direction these changes would take me.

Before I entered the whirlwind of cancer, I had been obsessed with having every facet of life in perfect order. I never left the house without looking perfect; my clothes and hair were just right, and of course I couldn't step foot out the door without makeup. I know it's vain, but that's a reflection of how insecure I truly was on the inside. I was always on time. My house was always clean and orderly. (Remember, we didn't have kids then!) There were never dishes in the sink or underwear on the floor,

His plan for my life had never been for me
to live in a state of desperation
and anguish. He wanted me to see myself
the way *he* sees me, for me to embrace
myself as the daughter of God
he created me to be.

and if everything wasn't in perfect order then I would be on the rampage until it was.

I had created a flawless façade—or so I thought. When anyone or anything rocked the boat of order and cleanliness, it tied my insides in knots, because I feared at any moment the boat might capsize. I was like a ticking bomb, liable to explode at any minute because of all the tension inside me as I struggled to maintain this counterfeit world.

The sad truth was, I had no idea how unhealthy my life had become, both internally and externally. I was blind to the damage being inflicted on my heart, mind, spirit, and body. *Was it really that important to have all the laundry finished or the house in immaculate condition every second of the day? Would my world crumble if I didn't wear makeup or fix my hair some days? Would the world come to an end if I didn't follow "the plan"?* And why was I so obsessed with portraying a flawless, spotless image of myself and my home? And most of all: What did these delusions really say about the root of my identity?

✿ ✿ ✿

Because of the spiritual journey God has taken me on through my years of dealing with the uncertainties and pains of breast cancer, I can now answer some of those questions. I was completely unaware before cancer that my self-worth and self-acceptance had been based on the way I was perceived by the world around me. I had no sense of self. I didn't know who I really was. God was about to take me on the ride of a lifetime, through which he would reveal his overwhelming love for me. He is persistent and unyielding in his effort to reveal his love to all of us. His plan for my life had never been for me to live in a state of desperation and anguish. He wanted me to see myself the way *he* sees me, for me to embrace myself as the daughter of God he created me to be. I believe he created all of us in his image with a specific plan and a purpose. We were all designed with a unique destiny that ultimately brings glory to him.

How did my experience with breast cancer bring about such an internal shift, revolutionizing my ideas about life? It started with the realization of how little control I have over my life. This is one of the first lessons for every cancer patient—whatever illusion of control over your life you thought you had is stripped away with that diagnosis.

God intended, through my cancer and the years of treatment to fight it, to show me life from a different vantage point. My perspective would shift—but not overnight. It would take a long and treacherous journey filled with many highs and lows. I don't think my experience is unique. For many of us, God uses a traumatic jolt like cancer, the death of a loved one, the loss of a job, or an awful breakup to awaken our hearts to who we truly are—to who he has made us to be. These tragic moments can be catalysts—they can create the revelation of our soul that drives us to embrace our identity in Christ.

My diagnosis forced me, very much against my will, into an unknown world. Up until that point in my life I had been comfortable with the orderly little world I had fabricated; it was safe, free from conflict, and smooth sailing. But God had a different plan in mind. Cancer completely blindsided me, but it was no surprise to God. He would use it to wreck me from the inside out—in the best way.

Chapter Five
New Normal

This wrecking of my heart and soul wasn't going to come without a lot of pain. The road ahead was going to be chock-full of growing pains. The process through which God refines our hearts is extremely hazardous and creates great vulnerability, but the journey yields an eternal return if we come alongside him and fully surrender ourselves to his will.

I was at a fork in the road of life. God was presenting me with a choice: Would I allow him to speak to me, stretch me, challenge me, change me, and make me new? Or was I going to resist his desire to overhaul my heart and mind and stay bound in the safe little prison I had created?

As the stress of finding a way to respond to that choice increased, so the stress increased in our home. I remember one evening Steve and I had come home from work and assumed the normal routine of dinner, watching a few television shows, shower, and off to bed. We sat quietly watching the screen, but the tension in the air you could cut with a knife. Steve didn't say anything. I didn't say anything.

Finally I got up from the couch and mumbled, "I'm going to take a shower and go to bed."

He followed me around the corner and down the hall. Then he said, "What's wrong? What's going on with you?"

I spun around and snapped, "If I *knew* what was wrong, then I would *tell* you what's wrong. I don't know."

But here's what I did know: Life as I'd known it before cancer was over. No matter how strong a woman you think you may be, nothing prepares you for hearing those words: *You have cancer.* No one takes a Cancer 101 class growing up. How can any of us know how we'll respond to any trauma in life until we've faced it head on? How do you accept having a disease living inside your body that threatens your life?

Unless you've traveled this road, it's hard to accurately comprehend and articulate how excruciating the journey is—physically as well as emotionally, spiritually, and relationally. Whether we have surgery, reconstruction, chemo, radiation, or any other form of therapy, it's an extended,

---

The process through which God refines our hearts is extremely hazardous and creates great vulnerability, but the journey yields an eternal return if we come alongside him and fully surrender ourselves to his will.

---

death-defying path. We each have our own story. Those stories tend to give cancer survivors more in common with each other than we have with those who've never traveled this path, and that can make it a very lonely path, surrounded by loved ones who, no matter how hard they try, can't grasp the totality of what we're experiencing.

Regardless of our diagnosis or treatment plan, every story is significant. Once we've trekked this dangerous path, we are forever changed ... for better or worse.

✿ ✿ ✿

We enter a "new normal" of life. The choice of how we are going to live in this "new normal" is ours to make, but one thing is certain: When we're faced with life-changing and even life-threatening situations like cancer, we show our true colors. The deepest and most characteristic parts of our souls rise to the surface through our words, actions, and feelings.

As I was discovering my "new normal," I had to come to terms with many new things. For instance, I had to get to know my new body. Waking up to those horrific scars every morning didn't make it easy to move forward. I was disgusted with what I saw. Remember, my internal filter was corrupt, so my false beliefs about my body and who I was as a person were being magnified a thousand times. The deception I was trapped in had tainted my ability to see the truth.

The best way to describe the conflict raging in my soul is that it was an internal tug-of-war. I was in a period of spiritual revival and awakening, but by this time in my recovery I was only at the beginning stages of that awakening—the conflicted, uncomfortable part, characterized by enormous tension. I didn't like the uncomfortable feelings this revival of my soul was triggering in my thoughts and emotions. And I'm afraid I often took it out on Steve.

I'm naturally an introvert. I'm tremendously introspective. I think a lot, but what I'm thinking and feeling doesn't always come out. From a young age, I had always been an optimist. I believe in the power of positive thinking. But in my recovery from surgery, my optimism became a form of denial. In trying to be positive and move forward with life, I was "stuffing" my emotions in the hope that it would help turn my life back toward "normal." If I acted normal, then surely things would be normal, right? In effect, I was lying to myself—the "normal" I had known before my diagnosis was now gone forever. Because of the web of lies I was telling myself and everyone else, I was forced to maintain the impression that everything was "fine." But spiritually and emotionally, I was anything but fine.

The truth was, I hated how I looked. I was mad that I had to go through this. I was grief-stricken that I had lost the most intimate part of my feminine body. The self-deprecating thoughts that even my façade of optimism couldn't hold at bay resulted in isolation and depression. When I came home from work, I would emotionally escape by getting lost in watching television or reading so that I didn't have to think or talk about all the turmoil waging war inside of me. I knew, intellectually, that I needed guidance, but the lies I had memorized over a lifetime made me resist reaching out and asking for help. I didn't want to be perceived as a "weak" woman, so I continued drifting farther and farther from the shore of reality.

My head told me I should be self-reliant—pull up my big-girl panties and kick this emotional upheaval. But my heart was broken in a million pieces. I tried time and time again to mentally coach myself through the emotional roller coaster, but the harder I tried to keep it together on the outside, the deeper I sank on the inside. *What should I do? How could I find my "new normal"?*

As I fell deeper and deeper into this emotional abyss, I began to isolate myself more and more from Steve, withdrawing as a form of self-preservation. I noticed we were starting to drift apart, just going through the motions of everyday life. Eventually came that evening in October of 2003 when, heading for the shower, I told him I just didn't know what was wrong.

Steve desperately wanted to help me. He would have done anything to take my pain away. The problem was that I didn't know how to articulate what I was feeling, not even to myself. As a result, I became very secluded. Gradually, I was slipping into a deep depression.

I had finished the reconstruction process by this time. I'd been hopeful that my spirits would change once I'd completed the reconstruction and had the implants in place, but internally I continued struggling with the same pattern of highs and lows. Externally, I continued to try to put on my happy face and keep moving forward, but Steve was on to me. He knew there was more going on inside than I was letting on.

This well of despondency was on the verge of erupting. At any given moment, I might feel a surge of rage, followed moments later by a crying episode. I had no idea what was going on inside of me. I felt like a crazy woman. Emotionally, I was spinning out of control, and I didn't know how to stop the spinning.

One morning, Steve and I were getting ready for work. I sat at the end of the bed while he was in the bathroom shaving. Even though I wasn't the best at verbal communication, I wanted to try to share my heart.

I said, "Honey, I just want you to know how much I appreciate everything you've done for me and the way you've gone above and beyond to care for me. You've been so patient and kind even when I've been short with you or impatient because of my own internal frustration. I know you don't deserve to be treated that way. I'm so sorry. Will you forgive me?"

He wiped his face and sat by me on the bed. He wrapped his arm around me and said tenderly, "Of course."

"I don't know what's wrong with me," I said. "I know I need help, but I'm embarrassed. I feel like I should be able to move past this. I know I should be grateful to be alive and healthy. I don't understand why I'm having such a hard time."

"No one knows how to cope with cancer," he said. "It's okay if you need to talk with someone. I don't want this battle to tear us apart. I can tell you've been pulling away from me because you don't know how to process everything you're going through inside. I will find someone you can talk to."

Steve pulled me into his arms, and we embraced for a long time. I finally felt like we were making a step in the right direction.

Chapter Six
The Beginning of Healing

After months and months of searching for the right counselor, Steve finally called me and said, "Babe, I found someone who can see us."

Rather than relief, I felt an immediate sense of panic. Even though I knew I needed help and I didn't want to feel this way anymore, I was still scared to death. Meeting with a counselor meant I would have to uncover my deepest wounds, the ones I concealed from everyone, even myself. The internal tug-of-war raged on. I felt as if my heart were ripping in two. Would the counselor be able to guide me to a breakthrough? Or would I simply stay the way I was?

"Her name is Annamarie Carter. She's a breast cancer survivor, too." he said, clearly relieved and excited to have found someone suitable.

"Really?" I said.

"She had a lateral mastectomy several years ago."

"How old is she? What are her credentials?" I was like a defense attorney, looking for any excuse why this wouldn't work. I was determined to find something wrong with her before I'd even met her. If I could discredit her, then I wouldn't have to go, right? Even though I desperately wanted to be free from the prison I was captive in, I wasn't sure I was ready to give up the comfort of privacy that prison deceptively offered me. It had become a security blanket, in some distorted way. I had grown comfortable with the lies I believed about myself. I know it sounds counterproductive to think this way, but it was almost easier to allow the lies to continue pulling me down than it was to make the vulnerable effort and exert the emotional energy it would take to break free.

What would the counselor think of me? Would Steve be able to accept me once he realized just how much perverted thinking was going on inside of me? Was I even capable of being honest with myself? Did I truly want to let go? Would I be able to lay down the cloak of despair and choose freedom?

Who goes to see a counselor—crazy people, right? What would people say when I dropped my disguise and they could see that I was mentally ill? Would I still be loved? Accepted? It would be days later, after a great deal of prayer and reflection, before I truly understood I needed to lay down my pride and fear of what other people would think of me if I went to a counselor. I would never know freedom, never learn who I really am and how God sees me, unless I was willing to face the fear head on and remove the veil of shame and rejection to embrace my true identity in Christ.

Steve continued: "Honey, she's the only person I've found who's right for us, after the dozens of calls I've made. We need to give her a chance. I know you're scared, but it's going to be okay. Let's give it a shot."

Steve wasn't willing to let me stay in this cage. He would make sure I went, even if he had to drag me there. My husband wasn't going to allow his wife to settle for "good enough" any longer, because he knew I was created for greatness.

Fear keeps us dormant and stagnant.
Bravery is making the step to move forward
in the midst of our fear.

Voice quavering, I said, "You're right. I'm just scared. I know I need to take this step if I want to be fully healed spiritually and emotionally."

Living in captivity to the deceptions I had surrounded myself with after surgery was exhausting. I was worn out from carrying on the act. It was time to take off the mask. If I wanted something different from the half-life I was living, then I would have to do something drastically different. If we want to overcome our fear, we must face it—not hide from it. How can we expect to get to the other side of the mountain if we're not willing to put in the work and endure the pain to climb the mountain? Fear keeps us dormant and stagnant. Bravery is making the step to move forward in the midst of our fear. We can't wait until the fear is gone. Fear dissipates in the face of courage.

As I took the courageous step to finally meet with her, I knew I was embarking on a journey of self-discovery and freedom. Growth can't come without pain. Just as I had endured the pain to have the cancer cut out of my body, it would also be painful to cut out the junk in my heart. God was showing me the parallel effects cancer can have—both physical and spiritual. These were, for me and for any cancer survivor, some of the growing pains of life. To become a healthy and whole woman—not just like before, but *better* than before—I would have to face my fear and lean into it.

❊ ❊ ❊

The day of the appointment came. I didn't know what to expect. I had never gone to a counselor before. Honestly, I had stereotyped both counselors and the "crazy" people who went to counselors. Little did I know God was about to shatter my misconceptions.

Steve and I pulled into the parking lot. My heart was beating at ninety miles an hour, and butterflies filled my stomach. As we walked cautiously to the entrance, I reached down with sweaty palms and grabbed Steve's hand for comfort. The thought of exposing the deepest part of my heart to a stranger was almost crippling. I knew I was on the front line of the war for my future. It was time to go to battle and fight for the freedom Christ had sacrificially died to offer me.

I hesitated at the door and almost turned around and ran for the car, but I was reminded God had plans for the rest of my life, and there was no more time to waste. I was ready to till up all the rotten roots that suffocated my spirit and kept me from seeing myself the way my Creator sees me. Not only did I want to embrace myself, but I also wanted to love myself.

The building was old and outdated. We walked down a narrow hallway lit with fluorescent lights. The smell of mothballs filled the air. We stood in front of her office door staring at her name, Annamarie Carter, engraved on a brass nameplate. I looked at Steve and said, "This is it."

"Go on in," he said. It was as if he were my escort into a new world.

We had arrived a couple of minutes early. Annamarie was still meeting with another client, so Steve and I waited patiently on the couch in the waiting area. The room was cozy. Even though the décor was old-fashioned, it was still warm and inviting, with a selection of snacks and hot beverages.

A couple minutes later, the office door opened and Annamarie escorted out her previous client. Annamarie was an older woman with short, blonde hair, red lipstick, and a quirky personality. Not what I had expected.

"You must be Sarah and Steve," she said with a huge smile.

"Yes, ma'am," I replied.

"Go ahead and get something to drink if you'd like, then take a seat inside. I'll be with you in a moment."

Steve and I walked into her office. It was dimly lit. The furnishings reminded me of something you would see in a grandmother's house—hunter-green walls with a mauve couch. We nestled onto the couch and sat in silence. You could hear a pin drop, it was so quiet.

Annamarie came in and settled comfortably into her chair. She placed her notepad on her lap. With a tender smile and soothing voice, she looked at me and said, "Tell me why you're here today."

I took a deep breath and gave her the general picture of my diagnosis and surgeries. "Since finishing the reconstructive surgery," I went on, "I've been having a hard time making sense of my emotions. I know I should be grateful the cancer isn't in my body anymore, but I can't seem to get past all the negative thoughts and feelings."

And I'd been worried about whether I'd be able to share at all! The thoughts and feelings rushed out of me like a waterfall. The pain of self-hatred I had carried, along with the lies that continually plagued my mind, drawing me deeper and deeper into hopelessness were beginning to rise to the surface. For the first time since my diagnosis, I was able to articulate the chaos in my head. The emotions I had bottled inside for so long were finally set free.

Honestly, I don't remember all I said that day. It probably didn't make a lick of sense, but the release I felt from letting everything out was revitalizing. Annamarie's validating nods and the comforting, supportive look in her eyes brought the soothing reassurance I had unknowingly longed for.

For eight months I had felt as if I were a foreigner in a strange land. I didn't know how to speak the language; no one understood me. Now, speaking to Annamarie, I finally felt someone understood the foreign language I had been speaking.

A huge weight had been lifted off my chest. I could finally breathe. I reached for a tissue on the coffee table. The tears streaming down my face were a cleansing flood washing away the pain. Annamarie and Steve sat in silence for several minutes while I soaked in the moment and received God's healing touch.

Annamarie eventually said, "Sarah, you're going through what we call a *grieving process*. Often amputees experience a grieving process for the loss of their body part much like the loss of a loved one. So many of us have experienced losses in our lives, but some of us haven't learned how to effectively grieve that loss and allow ourselves the freedom to move forward. We don't ever 'get over' grief, but we can learn to grieve well. That's what I want to teach you."

Still crying, I said, "Really? I've never heard of a grieving process. No one ever told me I would experience this kind of emotional roller coaster going through cancer."

"When I had my mastectomy," she said, "I went through a similar grieving process. At first I was angry, then I became sad, and over time I experienced each stage of grief. And there are definitely stages—predictable ones. I want you to know you're not alone and you're not crazy. This is absolutely normal."

"I don't feel normal."

"Once they've finished with their treatments or surgeries and they are trying to make sense of their new life, cancer patients experience a period of time we call 'finding your new normal.' What you're experiencing, and will experience, is a progression of healing. You learned to process and cope with emotion in a certain way, based on your childhood and life experiences. We all pick up unhealthy patterns. We don't know what we don't know. However, we can learn a new way of thinking and understanding that enables us to cope in a healthy way. I'm going to teach you a healthier way to identify and sort through your thoughts and emotions. This process is solely dependent on your willingness and effort to apply the principles we'll discuss. We won't get there overnight. You didn't learn your old method of coping in a day, so you're not going to relearn a new way in a short time either. This will be time consuming, but I promise in the end you will be a healthier and stronger woman."

Her insight and reassurances were so comforting—as was hearing her story. I began to feel that I *wasn't* crazy after all. Her ability to empathize with me was a wonderful gift.

Since I didn't know any other women who had breast cancer—and definitely no one my age—I didn't realize how comforting it was to have someone who could relate to my situation. It made all the difference in the world talking with someone who had already traveled this journey. It's not that my family and friends didn't love me and want to be there for me—they did. But what Annamarie offered was a different level of understanding and empathy that only comes with personal experience.

As that first session continued, she listened and allowed me the space to cry and let go of all the hidden hurts. She asked, "Have you allowed yourself time to say good-bye to your old body?"

"No, I didn't know I should."

"We'll sit here as long as it takes for you to cry it out," she said. "It's healing to release those tears and allow yourself to fully embrace each emotion you're experiencing."

"I didn't know how to do that," I said. "I thought I should just push the emotion down or ignore it in order to make it through the battle."

"It's healthy to allow your emotions to come out. That's how you begin the healing process. If you continually stuff your emotions, then you're stifling your ability to heal. You're denying your feelings if you don't express them in a healthy way. If we don't allow ourselves to grieve, then these emotions get bottled up, and eventually they'll explode."

As Annamarie and I talked, Steve sat listening intently. It was as if Annamarie was my interpreter. She translated to him what I was saying. Finally, he was beginning to understand the depth of the emotional war I had been fighting. He tenderly rubbed my back as I wiped my eyes. This session was the beginning of my healing.

❀ ❀ ❀

In my initial sessions with Annamarie, I had to go through a period of brokenness and humility. I had to admit I had no idea how to process and assimilate all the emotions and residual effects of cancer. Maybe it was my age. Maybe it was my upbringing. Maybe it was the experiences I had already been through in life that resulted in my dysfunctional perceptions. Or maybe it was simply my pride. Whatever the reason, it was time to take off the mask. I was so tired of feeling as if I was living someone else's life. I was ready to be me. It was time to allow the real Sarah to come alive.

For a year I met weekly with Annamarie. Steve came to every session with me. He was so supportive—not only in his willingness to attend the counseling sessions with me, but also in his understanding and his patience with me, as together we endured the long process of my getting well from the inside out. Since we are one, whatever I struggle with directly affects him, so we were committed to this journey together.

Annamarie guided me down a path that challenged me to explore my core beliefs of self-worth and identity. She didn't tell me what to believe or how to feel. Her questions pointed me in the right direction to discover my true self. God will use any method he chooses to enable us to see him and embrace his love for us. He used my time with Annamarie to awaken my soul and open my eyes to the way God sees me.

One sunny day, Annamarie closed the blinds to her office to block the heat and offer a more private and safe haven. We greeted each other as we usually did. Annamarie shifted in her seat, searching for a position that would alleviate her severe back pain. Once she was content, she straightened her bifocals and we started talking. At first we reviewed our previous session and recapped the things she had been teaching me. In recent weeks, we had been slowly digging deeper and deeper to the roots of my pain.

Annamarie asked, "Sarah, do you love yourself?"

"I think I do."

"Tell me what your self-talk sounds like. Are you kind to yourself? Do you beat yourself up?"

"Honestly, I've never consciously thought about it," I said. "But now that you ask, I guess I'm actually pretty hateful and berating toward myself."

"Why do you think you talk to yourself that way?"

My eyes welled with tears. I was being honest

> True beauty is dependent not on the shape of my body but on the shape of my soul—a soul crafted by God, infused with his love, equipped with his passion and purpose.

with myself about this for the first time—and it stung. "I guess, deep down, I don't love myself. I've treated myself as if I'm a failure and unworthy of unconditional love. I've always *tried* to say and do the right things to be worthy of love ... including God's love."

"Do you think God wants you to work for his love?" she asked.

"Well ... yes, I guess I do," I said.

"I want to challenge you to really spend time in prayer and ask God how he sees you," she suggested. I came home that afternoon and sat on my balcony of our apartment with a cold glass of sweet tea. As I leaned back in my Adirondack chair gazing at the clouds, I asked God, "How do you see me?"

You are royal. You are exceptional. I have made you in my image, God said, in a gentle whisper in my heart.

He was drawing me closer and closer to himself, gently luring me by his love. He knew how scared I was, but he also knew the victory that lay on the other side of this path of surrender. He wasn't willing to give up on me. He's not willing to give up on any of us.

In his Word, God tells us he came to bind up the brokenhearted and to set the captives free. The word *bind* means to wrap around something, to envelope or enfold, or to bandage. When God says he *binds* us, it means he wraps us in his love in order to heal us. Like a wounded and bleeding solider being wrapped tightly in bandages—that's what God desires to do to our hearts. He longs to come in and heal us, to set us free and release us to be fully known and make him known to a lost and hurting world. But in order to do that, we have the choice to allow him to fully take over our heart.

It took me a long time to give up the façade, to stop projecting the image that I knew how to deal with the journey of cancer. Instead, I had to accept my weakness and inability to handle the mental and emotional stress. The more honest I grew with myself, the softer my heart became. My grip was beginning to loosen.

When our hearts are soft and pliable, God can mold them to his image. He is the potter and we are the clay. When we bring our hurts to him, he changes us. The weakness we lay at his feet becomes the strength he imparts to heal us.

Was this process enjoyable? No. It was very painful. Each time I left Annamarie's office, it was as if my heart had been filleted. She was peeling back the layers of pain, hurt, dysfunction, and lies that had kept me captive for years and years. I was learning to be self-aware. After each session, I would spend time in prayer, asking God to reveal his perfect truth to my heart. This unveiling, although painful, was liberating my soul. It was as if I were meeting myself for the first time.

As I emerged from that grueling year of counseling, I saw myself and my identity in Christ in a whole new light. I understood true beauty is dependent not on the shape of my body but on the shape of my soul—a soul crafted by God, infused with his love, equipped with his passion and purpose.

I learned to see myself the way God sees me: loved unconditionally, immeasurably, and relentlessly. I now saw Steve's unyielding love as a constant reminder of God's love for me. I found myself truly believing I was not alone. Without a shadow of doubt I knew God was with me. Not only was he with me *now*, but he had always been there, and he was never going to leave me. His promise to us is that he will never leave us nor forsake us. There is absolutely nothing that can separate us from his perfect love. Not only is he with us, he is for us. He has good things in store for every one of us.

Of course, discovering these truths is one thing. Learning to walk in them takes practice, as I would soon learn. I had no idea of the challenges that, in the near future, would test these truths. But, thank God, my journey thus far had planted seeds of truth deep inside me. God was working his plan in my life. He would reveal his purposes for me in his perfect timing.

Chapter Seven
How Can I Make a Difference?

After my reconstructive surgery, Steve and I were finally in a less chaotic season of life. In fact, life was good. We purchased our first home—a three-bedroom gray brick home with a red door, built in 1974. We fell in love with this house. It had a huge backyard with a grand Bradford pear tree that shaded most of the yard. Behind the house was a greenbelt filled with trees. The perimeter of the yard was filled with beautiful flowers. Each morning I would enjoy my coffee under the arbor listening to the birds singing and the wind in the leaves. It was my own little paradise.

Sitting under the arbor, I would pray and listen to God. As I stilled my heart and invited God to speak, he would whisper words of love to my heart.

Sarah, I love you.

You're so beautiful to me.

I've created you to do great things.

I have good things in store for you.

These words of life were like a flood engulfing my soul. His love was equipping me with confidence and faith. Finally I was able to accept his encouragements and allow them into my heart. Before I would have dismissed his kindness and rationalized it as positive self-talk, but now that I was beginning to truly listen to the Holy Spirit, I could receive his love for me.

Even so, my heart ached—not for myself, but for the many thousands of women in the same boat I was in—facing cancer treatment, but without the kind of support I was finding now. I wept for marriages I knew were crumbling, for the women whose lives were being stolen by this disease, for the women who desperately wanted to have children but had now been robbed of their ability to conceive, for the

---

My heart ached—not for myself, but for the many thousands of women in the same boat I was in—facing cancer treatment, but without the kind of support I was finding now. I wept for marriages I knew were crumbling, for the women whose lives were being stolen by this disease, for the women who desperately wanted to have children but had now been robbed of their ability to conceive, for the husbands and children left behind after their wife and mother had stepped into eternity.

---

husbands and children left behind after their wife and mother had stepped into eternity. I couldn't sit idly by—and yet what could I do? How could I make a difference? How could I give back?

One evening after work I sat in my Adirondack chair under the arbor in my backyard. The sun was setting. A gentle breeze was blowing. I closed my eyes and listened to the birds singing; I felt the wind on my face. In that moment of serenity, I asked God: *How can I make a difference in this world? My heart breaks for women struggling with their treatment for breast cancer—but what can I do?* Gradually, ideas started coming to mind.

If money were no object, I asked myself, *what would I do?*

- I would provide the financial means to other women to give them the opportunity I had to spend one-on-one time with a counselor, so that they would be equipped with the coping skills to walk through this journey without being destroyed by it and left beside the road of life to rot.
- I would start a community of survivors to offer hope and encouragement to each other.
- I would put tools in the hands of these women to equip them for their battle.
- I would educate young women about the importance of self-exams and teach them how to do them.
- I would buy a beach house and offer retreats for survivors and their families.

- I would create safe environments for people to be vulnerable and shed their pain and be restored with healing.

And how would I do all this?
Late one evening, Steve and I were lying in bed. He was watching ESPN, as usual, and I lay there staring at the screen but preoccupied with the vision stirring inside of me. "Honey, I've been thinking about an idea," I said.

Only half listening, he said, "Oh yeah? What were you thinking?"

"I'd like to start a program—maybe a foundation or a nonprofit of some sort—to provide financial scholarships to other breast cancer survivors and their families to go to counseling. It's been life changing for us, and I'm sure other women would benefit too, if they had the chance—but it's so expensive. We know what it's like to be swamped with medical bills and yet not have our full salary because we're on medical leave. I think this would really help people."

His eyes brightened, and he sat up in bed. "I think that's an amazing idea."

"You do?"

"Absolutely. I agree with everything you said—this could be life changing for so many families. We had no clue how to cope with the grief and the emotional roller coaster your diagnosis and treatment brought. We wouldn't be where we are today if we hadn't spent time with Annamarie, equipping ourselves with new skills. I think it would be awesome to provide this opportunity to others."

"Wow—I'm glad you're so excited! I wasn't sure what you would think. But how would we do this? Where should we start?"

"Well," he said, "maybe the first thing is to look at starting a nonprofit, so we have an identity and can accept donations. I'll call our accountant in the morning."

When we finished talking, I closed my eyes and drifted off to sleep, thinking of the amazing things that could happen if this dream became a reality.

I spent the next couple of weeks thinking about ways we could raise some money to get started. But the more I thought, the more anxious I became. How would I do this? I had no idea how to raise money. Would anyone donate toward this cause? And was this idea even worth our time and effort? My fear was almost paralyzing. Who was I to champion this cause?

Then God gently reminded me it wasn't about me. It was about him. He hadn't given me the idea for my own benefit. He'd given it to me to help others and bring glory to him. My heart was immediately filled with his peace. I knew I was moving in the right direction, and I was suddenly convinced I didn't need to worry about the details. I needed to trust him and to be obedient to his leading—and that's all. It's a scary thing to leave everything and follow the plan God has for our lives. It's hard for our carnal minds to rationalize some of things he asks us to do. That's why making the choice to trust his goodness and sovereignty builds our faith. We won't know everything. We're not God; that's why he tells us to walk by faith and not by sight. He shows us what we need to know when we need to know it.

Honestly, if he did reveal to us the entire masterpiece of his plan for our lives, we would probably be so overwhelmed we would stop dead in our tracks. Our role is to walk in obedience, one step at a time. His Word says if we love him, then we will obey him. My heart was fully surrendered to whatever God had in mind for me. I didn't know exactly how this idea he had given me would play out, but I knew the character of God, and he had never failed me. Even though things didn't always work out the way I thought they should, he had always been faithful. How could I do anything but obey?

The day of the meeting with our accountant, Steve and I walked up the path to her office in a quaint little house. The receptionist greeted us and escorted us to Lynne's office.

I started by saying, "I'm excited to share our idea with you and get some advice."

Lynne peered over the top of her glasses as I explained. Then she said, "This sounds like a fantastic idea. I'd love to help you get established. I can set up the business and get the IRS documents prepared for you. We're looking at around $1,500 to get started."

"Okay, let's get the ball rolling," Steve said with excitement and pulled out the checkbook.

In me, the emotion was not excitement but panic. *Are we really going to write a check right now?* I thought. *Are we ready for this? We have no idea what we're doing.*

We were walking into uncharted territory—at least for us. And inside, my feelings were completely contradictory. Was I ready to take the bull by the horns? Absolutely. Was I scared out of my wits and wanting to pull the chain to stop the bus before it went any further? You bet. Does that make sense? As I said before, for most of my life I've been terrified of the unknown and certainly no risk-taker. But this time was different. Despite my panic, it was as if a wind were pushing me forward, and I couldn't hold myself back. I was moving forward whether I wanted to or not.

"You'll need to come up with a name for the organization," Lynne said.

"I'd like to call it Project31." I've always loved the thirty-first chapter of the book of Proverbs in the Bible. It talks about a woman of noble character and her attributes. One verse in particular resonated with me: "Charm is deceptive, and *beauty is fleeting*; but a woman who fears the LORD is to be praised" (Proverbs 31:30 NIV, emphasis added). That summarized the desires of my heart. I loved God, and I wanted my life to illuminate his presence. So I decided to name the organization Project31 after this noble woman I aspired to emulate.

We wrote the check out of our savings—a major faith step for us. We weren't sure exactly where we were going, but we knew God did. We were simply responding to his promptings.

Our next step was to raise the initial $1500. I decided it would be fun to host a vision luncheon at a charming little café called Raspberries n' Crème. I would invite my closest friends, share my heart, and ask them to support me in this.

Over the next month I made catering arrangements, sent invitations, and made favor boxes for each guest with pink M&M's inside cute little white boxes tied with dainty ribbons. I picked out the perfect outfit and prepared my thoughts to share. I spent the whole month trying to craft the perfect presentation of my vision for Project31.

The night before the luncheon, I stood in front of the mirror practicing what I would say. I hated public speaking, but I was on a mission—there was a greater purpose at stake, and I would have to overcome my fears. This was only one of many hurdles I would have to jump over—one step at a time, one foot in front of the other.

"You can do this, Sarah," I told myself in the mirror. "Look how far you've come. You didn't come this far for nothing. You are called and equipped by God to do his work. He has a plan for you to be a beacon of hope to women."

I washed my face and got ready for bed. I was excited and terrified at the same time.

The next morning I got up early to make sure I had everything ready. I took my time getting ready. The butterflies in my stomach wouldn't calm down. I stood in front of the mirror and took some deep breaths to still my anxious heart.

At the café, before everyone arrived, I walked around the room, checking everything. The room was actually very small, and the long, rectangular tables had been arranged for maximum seating capacity, so there wasn't much room to move around. Each table had a freshly starched white tablecloth with turquoise and hot pink napkins. The smell of fresh flowers filled the room, and warm sunlight poured in. At the front of the room was a long, turquoise curtain—the backdrop for the speaking area. I had a black choir stand as my podium and a black stool.

I greeted the ladies as they arrived. Butterflies continued fluttering in my stomach as lunch was served. I ate barely anything. As the waitresses cleared the tables and prepared to serve our dessert, Steve stepped up to the speaking area and greeted everyone. As I sat listening to my husband speak so highly of me in his introduction, I could barely breathe. My palms were damp and there was a lump in my throat as I approached the front of the room. Steve gave me a warm embrace as if to say, "You can do this. I believe in you." Then he handed me the microphone.

This was it—my first time to share my heart and vision for Project31 in front of a group of people other than my family. I opened my mouth and the words started flowing. I don't remember exactly what I said. I just allowed my heart to do the speaking. Scanning the room as I spoke, trying to maintain eye contact with each woman for at least a few seconds, I watched one after another begin to cry. I could tell that what I was saying was touching their hearts.

As I finished, the women broke into applause. I couldn't stop smiling. Not only had I overcome a significant fear, but more than that, the vision God had given me resonated with them. God was stirring the hearts of these women to take action. We had placed a donation box by the exit in case anyone wanted to make a donation as they left that day, and when we got home, I counted the money. We had raised $2500 that day alone. What a huge blessing. We had enough money to establish our 501(c)3 status with the IRS, which would make us a legitimate nonprofit organization and allow us to accept tax-deductible donations. I couldn't believe it was actually happening. God was continuing to show us his faithfulness as we obeyed his direction.

I was gaining confidence. As God continued to reveal my true identity in him, I knew whose I was. He had me in the palm of his hand, and he would not lead me to a place he didn't want me to go. More than anything, I wanted to walk in the fullness God had for me. I didn't want to merely exist. I wanted to fulfill the calling God made me for. And he was opening doors right before my eyes.

All the junk we go through in our journey through breast cancer isn't for nothing—even though you may find yourself feeling that way at the lowest moments. But he has a plan for me and a plan for you. He can bring good things out of disasters. He is always faithful. The question is, *are we willing to persevere and trust him to reveal his plan?*

Chapter Eight
Adventure

One of my passions is to equip young women to be their own health advocates, especially regarding breast cancer. And that's what drew me one night to an event sponsored by the Oklahoma State University Panhellenic. There were about 450 sorority girls in attendance that evening. We met in an old banquet hall, with ancient wood floors that creaked; the air smelled of dust and old books. Steve and I had gotten there a little early, and since the room was empty I walked up and down the rows, taking in the smell and feel of the room, trying to calm my nerves.

The host introduced me, and I slowly made my way to the podium. I'd worn heels that night. Wearing heels gives me a sense of confidence. However, I hadn't stopped to consider I would be standing at a podium for a long time. Knocking knees and heels don't make a good combination.

I took the microphone from the host and faced the crowd. My knees wouldn't stop wobbling. I was so nervous I could barely stand, and my hands were so sweaty I was fearful of dropping the microphone. My eyes welled with tears. My voice was shaky. Would I be able to do this? *I'm making a fool of myself*, I thought. *How embarrassing.*

I decided to just be honest and be myself. I had nothing to lose. I walked to the front of the stage and sat down, feet dangling. "Is it okay if I just sit right here?" I said to the girls, laughing. "I confess—I'm nervous." And I was, but this was part of my training. One of my mentors had encouraged me to share my story as much as I could. He said the more I shared it out loud, the better I would be at articulating my journey. Early on, I could barely get through my story without a crying fest. But the more I said it out loud, the more I could tell God was mending my brokenness. By the time of the OSU presentation, I would still have short moments where I would tear up, but I wouldn't be completely overwhelmed with emotion anymore.

Once I was seated on the stage, I felt more comfortable. I began to tell the story, in the third person, of a young woman who developed breast cancer. I described the challenges she went through, the medical setbacks, the pressure on her marriage, and her struggle to love herself. When I came to the end of the story, I looked out over the crowd and slowly said, "And that young woman … was me."

Gasps and cries erupted. One girl got up and ran out.

I had told my story in the third person before, and had discovered it gave the presentation a more dramatic effect. Most people don't think someone my age could have breast cancer, so their response when I reveal that it's my story is normally disbelief and a sense of harsh awakening as they realize it could as easily have been them. Cancer doesn't affect just older women.

That night, though, I admit I was a little overwhelmed by their responses. I hadn't expected them to get so upset.

We will never grow if we don't face our fears. Fear always holds us back.

When the program was over, I lingered in front of the stage and several girls came up to talk with me. It was humbling to see how much impact my personal journey can have on someone else's life.

God was reminding me how powerful the words of our testimony can be. He's writing a story through each one of us. We can choose to open our mouths and allow our words to breathe life into those around us through God's power ... or not.

Slowly, I was becoming more comfortable with being in front of groups—something I had thought might never happen. I had read public speaking is the number-one fear of American adults! I believe it, because it had certainly been a major fear for me. I clearly wasn't doing this out of my own strength. This was God's strength working in me. His strength is always made perfect in our weakness. Despite my terror of getting up in front of people, I knew I needed to lean into that fear and allow God to stretch me and continue taking me to a deeper level of trust with him. We will never grow if we don't face our fears. Fear always holds us back.

✿ ✿ ✿

We continued raising funds for Project31. Each time we raised a little money, God would present another opportunity. We jumped at every chance we had to share our story. And I was up to the challenge, feeling strong both physically and emotionally.

At least I was feeling strong until one morning in February of 2004, when I woke up not feeling like myself. I was dizzy. My head ached.

Since my surgeries, my menstrual cycles had gotten out of whack. I tried to remember the last time I'd had a period. It had been at least nine weeks. *Could I be pregnant?*

The oncologist had advised us to wait to start a family for at least two years. But, they explained, since they'd never had a patient so young before, they didn't know how to advise me, so they were being cautious. Steve and I listened to their advice, but we knew God had a plan for us, and we would have children in his time.

I decided to wait until after work that day to run by the store and buy a pregnancy test. I got home around 5:45—Steve would be home in thirty minutes. I ran to the bathroom and peed on the stick, then sat anxiously waiting for two minutes—would *one* or *two* lines pop up?

Slowly one pink line emerged.

I waited a couple more seconds.

What is that? Another line faintly appeared.

Could it be? Am I pregnant? My heart started racing. *Oh, my gosh—I'll take the other test just to be sure.*

Feverishly, I unwrapped the second test, got the stick out, and repeated the procedure. Then I closed my eyes and waited.

By the time a minute had gone by, I couldn't take it any longer. I had to look. I opened my eyes—and there it was: two *bright* pink lines staring back at me.

Despite the two tests, I still couldn't believe it. I was in awe.

I took a few deep breaths and calmed my heart rate. Steve would be home any minute. I sat on the bathroom floor, restlessly waiting for him to get there. How should I tell him? What would I say? Would he be excited?

I heard his old pickup pull into the driveway. When I heard the door from the garage to the kitchen open, I stood, grabbed the stick, and walked from the bathroom to the living room. Steve had just lain down on the couch to rest.

I had the test behind my back as I entered the room. "Guess what?" I said, but before he could respond, I blurted, "I'm pregnant!" I held up the test.

Shocked and speechless, he sat there for a moment. I sat beside him, and we just stared at each other in amazement. Wow—we were going to be parents! Finally Steve recovered enough to lean closer and give me a big hug. "I'm so excited," he said. "This is awesome!"

With tears in my eyes, I said, "This is wild. I can't believe it. I'm going to be a mom. You're going to be a dad."

Most couples are excited and awed when they first discover they're pregnant. But for breast cancer survivors, it's a unique thrill—and relief—and cause for concern. I was so grateful for the opportunity to have a child. It was a gift to be able to conceive. I had known we might have trouble conceiving due to cancer. But we *had* conceived, which made us privileged among cancer survivors. Because of the extreme effects of some of the treatments used for breast cancer, some women's bodies become infertile. It's a devastating reality far too many of us face.

The inability to bear a child can paralyze some women emotionally and psychologically. Only those who have had this possibility stripped from them understand the level of pain these women endure and the level of grief they experience. It is nothing less than heart wrenching.

To be created by God as women with the capacity to conceive, to carry, and to birth another human being is a miraculous privilege and blessing. Those of us who have experienced that blessing, let us not forget our sisters who are suffering because they were denied it by the effects of their cancer. May we be sensitive and compassionate in their time of anguish.

Steve and I, aware of the risks we had faced, were beyond grateful to be allowed to experience this gift. But we had no idea what we were doing, like every new parent.

In unknown territory, God promises to be a lamp unto our feet and a light unto our path. There's a reason why we can't see the entire path in front of us. If we could, then it wouldn't involve faith, and we wouldn't need God. Our limited vision creates a dependence on him that continually lures us back into relationship with him. Without him, we walk blindly in darkness.

He promises to restore the brokenhearted. *To restore* means to bring back to a former, original, or normal condition—to reestablish. He wants to reconstruct the areas of loss and pain we've experienced in life. We might not get back specifically what we've lost, but God can come into our most broken places and mend our soul. He wants to make us better than new.

The road to healing looks different for everyone. For some of us, healing might be immediate, or nearly so. For others, it's a process, and that process might take far longer than we wish it would. That's up to God—and our willingness to cooperate with his promptings and fully trust him with the process. It's vital to invite him into every facet of the journey, and ask him to open our eyes to his leading.

It was amazing to watch the Holy Spirit move in my life and Steve's when we asked him to open our eyes. Too often, we go through life with blinders on, and we become so laser focused with our to-do list that we forget to slow down and invite him to be our guide and reveal himself to us.

We treasured our little Colin and enjoyed every moment of parenting him. One afternoon when he was still a toddler and I was trying to wind down after a trying day at work, I was sitting on the couch watching him play. I felt more exhausted than usual. Suddenly I wondered: When had my last period been? At least five weeks ago....*Could I be pregnant again? No way!*

I rummaged through the bathroom cabinet until I found the extra tests leftover from when I found out I was pregnant with Colin. I went to the bathroom to take the test and then left it on the bathroom counter and went back to the living room to play with Colin—an attempt to distract myself so I wouldn't get too anxious. Five minutes later, I went back into the bathroom, peeked at the stick—and there were two *bright* pink lines staring me in the face again! I couldn't believe it!

I wept—only partly for joy. I knew that this was an incredible blessing, but I also felt completely overwhelmed.

I was wiping my tears when I heard the door from the garage open into the kitchen. Steve walked into the living room, excited as usual to see us.

"Hi, rock star!" he said as Colin crawled toward him. Then he looked at my face and said, "Hi, Babe—what's wrong?"

Through tear-filled eyes, I said, "I'm *pregnant*."

"Are you serious?" he said, excited.

"I can't believe it," I said.

He sat down next to me and put his arm around me. "Why are you upset? This is awesome."

"I just feel bad for Colin. He's just a baby. It's not fair to him."

"Honey, I'm sure Colin won't look at it that way. This will be an addition to our family. He'll have a little sister or little brother to play with."

"I know," I said. "I guess I'm just in shock. I just need some time to process."

He rubbed my back and said, "We'll be okay. This is a wonderful blessing. Let's be thankful."

Once again, God was taking us into new territory. The adventure never ends with God. Just when we think we've got it figured out, BAM! He's always got another surprise up his sleeve.

I like the way author Mark Batterson describes the life of someone following the Holy Spirit. He equates it to chasing a wild goose—in fact, he wrote a book called *Wild Good Chase*. He wrote:

We try to make God fit within the confines of our cerebral cortex. We try to reduce the will of God to the logical limits of our left-brain. But the will of God is neither logical nor linear. It is downright confusing and complicated.

A part of us feels as if something is spiritually wrong with us when we experience *circumstantial uncertainty*. But that is precisely what Jesus promised us when we are born of the Spirit and start following Him. *Most of us will have no idea where we are going most of the time.* And I know that is unsettling. But circumstantial uncertainty also goes by another name: adventure. (From *Wild Goose Chase: Reclaim the Adventure of Pursuing God*, by Mark Batterson. Colorado Springs, CO: Multnomah, 2008, p. 2)

On the morning of March 17, 2006—St. Patrick's Day—we arrived at the hospital around 7:30 a.m. By noon, it was time to push. The nurses pulled the stirrups out of the bed and got everything ready. Steve was right by my side, holding my leg. I pushed with all my might, and our baby girl made her arrival in less than ten minutes. She was precious. She nestled her head under my chin. I patted her bottom and whispered, "I love you, Tatum. You're our little good luck charm."

Chapter Nine
Slow Down

How time flies once you have children! It had been hard enough to keep up with the demands of life *before* children. What was I thinking? We tried our best, but between the demands of work and the ebb and flow of each new season of parenthood, life was stressful.

One day I came home from a particularly stressful day at work. I got the kids a snack and went to my bedroom to change into some sweats. When I got to the bathroom, though, I sat down on the floor to breathe deeply and calm my anxious heart. Leaning back against the tub, I closed my eyes, drew my knees into my chest and let my head sink onto them. Soon, tears were streaming from my eyes. I felt pulled in a million different directions. How could I continue at this pace? I had so many things to get done. And yet I knew tons of moms who, it appeared to me, were able to do so much more. What was wrong with me?

Then I felt the touch of a little hand on my shoulder, and a high voice said, "Mommy, you okay?"

I raised my head, wiped my tears, and pulled Tatum to me. "Yes, baby, Mommy is okay."

But actually, I wasn't. I was so exhausted I felt I had little or nothing left to give, even to this precious little one. My position at church was executive

---

I felt like I was on a treadmill that was gradually getting faster and faster. It was becoming too much to bear. I had no margin in my life. I was exhausted and on the verge of burnout.

---

assistant to the senior pastor, a position that required a lot of emotional energy all day every day, caring for the needs of someone else. After work I would come home to my second full-time job caring for my little ones. Steve was gone a lot, coaching baseball, and I was slowly becoming overwhelmed by all the day-to-day responsibilities required to keep a household with two small children functioning. I felt like I was on a treadmill that was gradually getting faster and faster. It was becoming too much to bear. I had no margin in my life. I was exhausted and on the verge of burnout.

And I knew better. I should not have allowed this situation to sneak up on me. Even after everything God had already been teaching me, I was losing myself in the hustle of everyday life. Without realizing it, I had stopped making myself a priority.

One of the hardest lessons I had learned along my journey with cancer was to give myself permission to put myself *first*—not selfishly, but in a way that reflected my position in the overall system of our family and in the eyes of the Lord.

The second-greatest commandment, Jesus reminded the Pharisees, is to love others as we love ourselves. It's impossible to love others if we don't love ourselves. And part of loving ourselves well is making time to care for ourselves first. If we believe that Christ loved us enough to die for us, then we have to believe that we are worth the effort of caring for. We're only able to love others well out of the overflow of our own wellness.

It's like the safety mask illustration. Before a flight takes off, the flight attendant stands and goes through the safety precaution speech. She explains that, in case of emergency, the oxygen masks will drop from the ceiling—and you must secure your own mask *first* before attempting to help those around you.

We have to *choose* to be gracious to ourselves. If we don't value ourselves by doing whatever it takes to ensure that we remain whole and healthy, then no one can do it for us. And if we don't make that choice, how can we adequately care for our families, friends, and loved ones? How can we be the best employee we're capable of being? How can we impact the world with our unique gifts and talents? How can we make a difference?

That's why I needed to put myself at the top of my own priority list. God was challenging me to evaluate *all* my priorities. It's important, after going through a life-threatening situation like cancer, to reevaluate what is truly important to us at our core.

Most of us spend our lives at war with an onslaught of demands on our time and money. Our culture tries to dictate how we're going to spend our resources. Some of us get sucked into the deception that the formula for peace, intimacy, and joy includes:

- more stuff
- more success
- more status
- more fame
- more exposure
- more accomplishments

None of those things can take the place of relationships. We are relational beings, created for community. So it's not satisfying when we find ourselves, as so many of us do, drowning in a sea of debt trying to pay for all the stuff we worked so hard to give our family to make them happy. The reality is that they didn't need more *stuff*—they really needed more of us. But to create margin in our lives so that we can spend more time with our loved ones, we have to decide what we can sacrifice. *Where can I make more time for my family? How can I carve out time to spend with others?* The sad thing is that it takes something like cancer for some of us to wake up to this.

An honest inventory of your schedule and bank accounts would probably reveal that *your use of time and money already reflects your true priorities.* If we say our family is the most important thing to us, are we making the best investment of our time toward building intimacy with them? In the stress and burnout I was feeling on that day when I sat and wept on the bathroom floor, God was prompting me to assess my use of time. Was my life an accurate reflection of my priorities?

Tatum touched her tiny fingertip to my wet cheek and asked, "What wrong, Mommy?"

"Mommy's a little sad," I said.

She laid her head on my chest and said, "It's okay, Mommy. I wuv you."

I hope you're right, I thought. *I hope it's going to be okay.* With my eyes closed, I caressed her hair and said, "I love you too, baby girl."

With my priorities so far out of whack, I was experiencing fatigue to such an extent that I was nearly dysfunctional. After working so hard to become healthier since my surgeries, I felt like I was back at square one.

Not only was I not adequately loving myself or my family, I also wasn't making intentional time for God the way I had been before the kids were born. I had put him on the back burner. I'm embarrassed to admit this, especially after everything he had already done for me, but my work at the church had started to substitute for daily time with God. I was so overwhelmed—my schedule was so full and my time so limited—that I had begun to think I was maximizing my use of time by allowing my work to "count" as my personal time with God. How could I have been so naïve and deceived? Why would I think that my career as a "professional Christian" could ever take the place of sitting at the feet of my Savior and spending one-on-one time with him?

And yet even as I tried to put God in a box and check him off the to-do list, he still pursued me. His love is unconditional. There's nothing we can do or not do, nothing we can say or not say, that will ever take his everlasting love away from us. His love is steadfast. It's the same yesterday, today, and forever. Regardless of how many ups and downs I was going through, one thing was certain: he would never leave me.

Even after that morning with Tatum on the bathroom floor, I continued working full-time at the church in addition to taking care of the kids and the house and building Project31. The church was growing rapidly, and the demands of my job were ever increasing. I tried my best to be the best wife, mother, and employee, but my inner resources were strained far beyond their limit.

I became conscious of an unsettling in my spirit—a stirring that told me something was about to change. One morning after dropping the kids off at church-staff childcare, which was upstairs from my office, I rushed down the stairs to get to my desk and start the day. Mid-step, I heard God say in my spirit, *Slow down.*

"What?" I said.

You're in too big of a hurry. You need to slow down, he said.

"What do you mean?"

I didn't create you to live at the pace you're trying to maintain. I need you to slow down and walk with me.

His words had already had an effect. I was taking the stairs slowly, one step at a time. At the bottom of the staircase, just before I opened my office door, I took a deep breath and said, "Please show me how. I don't know how to do that."

And he did. Over the next couple of months, I continued to talk with God about what he meant when he said *slow down.* He revealed an incredible truth to me: There was more. More healing. More restoration. More intimacy—all of these were things he wanted to make known to me. Our God is a God of *more than enough.* There's always more with God. He never runs dry. He's continually drawing us to deeper and deeper places of intimacy with him, but it's critical that we *slow down*—that we spend time with him and allow him full access to our hearts.

I sensed him saying over and over again that he didn't care how much I produced for him. He didn't care how busy I made myself—even doing things for him. He didn't care how well I performed or how successful I became. What he cared most about was how much time I spent with him. He cares about being with me! And he cares about being with you. But we're too busy, too distracted, too caught up in our own world, so we don't *slow down* to hear his whispers.

He longs to be with us. But since it's in the stillness where we meet him, *how can we hear him and find him in that stillness if we don't slow down?* Because it's God who provides the abundance in our lives, we live fully only to the extent that we experience intimacy with the Father. He desires for us to walk in the fullness of life, but that's impossible apart from him.

The greatest commandment is to love God with all of our heart, soul, mind, and strength. After that he says to love others as we love ourselves. If I wanted to love God with all my heart, soul, mind, and strength, then I would have to make some significant changes in my life. I would have to slow down. If I wanted to walk in rhythm with God, then I would need to reexamine my priorities.

On a Thursday afternoon in December, I sat in my boss's office in a chair framed in chrome with a black leather seat. He sat in his metal-framed, leather-upholstered rocking chair behind the huge, rustic, wooden table that served as his desk. Normally he left around 3:45 p.m. to go to the gym, and before he left, we always went through our to-do list. The sun shone brightly through the windows behind him. After we had finished the list, I said, "I have one more thing. I've made a big decision."

He looked back at me, puzzled.

I had spent the past eight and a half years in this position. I had dedicated a lot of my life to serving the church. Now was the time to let go and trust God's leading.

"You know I love working for you. You know I love the church. You also know how I've been struggling. I've decided I need to make a change in order to bring peace back into my home."

His eyes now, like mine, started to well with tears—he sensed what I was about to say.

"I can't do it anymore. I have to put my family first. My husband and children need me, and I'm not able to give them all of me because I'm stretched too thin. It's been my honor to work for you as long as I have. You have taught me so many things that have forever changed me."

Our God is a God of *more than enough*.
There's always more with God.
He never runs dry.

"Sarah, you are an extraordinary woman. You've done an amazing job serving me for so long. You, Steve, and the kids have been family to us, and you always will be. You've been through so much. It's been incredible to watch God work in your life."

We both sat and cried. This was a transitional moment for both of us. His world and mine were both about to change in dramatic ways.

"I'll miss working with you," he said.

"Me too."

I would still need to work, and we discussed other positions in the church, less stressful and demanding, that I could move into. I chose one in another department.

After that, our lives slowed considerably. It was refreshing to take our time and not feel like we were running a race every morning. I finally understood the value of slowing down. As we set new standards for ourselves and made a conscious effort to protect our family time, God continued to heal our souls and knit our hearts closer together.

My passion for Project31, however, intensified. Now that I had margin, I was able to concentrate more on cultivating my desire to encourage and empower women. One day, at the suggestion of my dear friend Jane, another breast cancer survivor, I had lunch with Becky Lowery, the genetic counselor at the breast imaging center where I was diagnosed. Her boss, Tracy Cothran, director of the center, joined us at the Panera Bread across the hospital. They were delightful—their interaction reminded me of Lucy and Ethel from *I Love Lucy*. They made me laugh. As we got to know one another that day, I shared my journey and my passion to restore women. They asked a ton of questions, and their questions revealed that they longed to develop a support system for their patients. I asked why they hadn't started a support group already. They knew the need was great, they said, but they believed that a peer-led group would be more effective. They simply hadn't yet met the right person to lead a group.

The thought of creating, developing, and nurturing a community of survivors excited me greatly. I confess that, immediately after my surgery, I had dismissed support groups as places where women would come to wallow in their misery and feed a toxic monster. Not until I had personally benefitted from counseling did I realize the need for education, awareness, and comfort from fellow survivors.

Impulsively I blurted, "I'll do it! I'll start a support group for you. Jane and I can colead."

"Are you serious?" Becky replied.

"Absolutely."

Both of them were ecstatic that I was willing to create a healthy peer-to-peer support group model. Over the next month, we settled on a time, date, location, and topic. We sent out communication to all local breast imaging centers, oncology offices, and hospitals.

And so in March of 2011 we launched our first Project31 support group. Our first meeting was unforgettable. Jane and I had decided to start the evening by sharing the vision and mission of Project31. We explained to the ladies that we wanted to create a safe and loving environment where women and their families can be embraced, equipped, and empowered to live fully restored lives. The ladies were hungry to connect with other women who understood on an intimate level what they were walking through. I had been worried whether the ladies would feel comfortable enough to open up. We couldn't get them to stop talking! It was incredible to watch a community being born.

That night God revealed another step in his plan for Project31. He was calling us to build a community of survivors to comfort and uplift one other—to inspire hope.

The support groups weren't the only means by which Project31 was reaching out, though. About a year before we began the groups, I had been trying to think of ways I could create something to put in the hands of survivors. I knew that some women would be open to going to a counselor, but others might not, and some might not even be willing to attend a support group. I remembered that when I was first diagnosed, I wasn't ready to interact with a support group—but I might have been willing to read a book on my own. That's when God gave me the idea for something we called Handbag of Hope.

It's simply a tote bag with helpful resources that introduce a survivor to the healing journey. I cater each bag to the recipient's specific needs, but in general, a bag includes a cookbook with cancer-fighting recipes, a book about life after breast cancer, a book for husbands, a spiritual journal, a Project31 T-shirt, and a brochure to introduce them to our organization and, we hope, give them a connection point if and when they ever want to talk to someone. Project31 was growing!

Chapter Ten
Déjà Vu

My annual checkup at the breast imaging center was scheduled for August 1, 2011, and I arrived about 1:30 p.m. Since my reconstructive surgery, the doctor had advised me to have annual MRIs to check on my implants.

When I checked in, the receptionist asked, "Have you noticed any changes since your last visit?" It was a question I could easily answer, because I had continued to do self-exams—even though I'd *had* a double mastectomy. It's impossible for surgeons to get every single microscopic cell. And, as a matter of fact, I had noticed a change. About five months before, I had noticed a spot on my ribs on my right side. I hadn't paid much attention to it, thinking that it was probably just scar tissue from all the surgeries. I told the receptionist about it. She said, "Wait here while I call down to the radiologist. She may want to do an ultrasound before we do the MRI."

I sat in the waiting room while she made the call. A few minutes later, she called my name. "The doctor wants to have the ultrasound when you're finished with the MRI. Have a seat and the nurse will call you back shortly."

Soon the nurse led me back to the dressing room, where I changed clothes and, not wanting to go through the ultrasound alone, feverishly tried to get hold of Steve. I had unpleasant memories of having gone through the first one by myself. I kept calling but got no answer. He coaches not just baseball but football too, and he normally doesn't hear his phone in the afternoons while he's coaching. Finally I just left a message, hoping he would get it while I was having the MRI and maybe get here before the ultrasound.

The MRI lasted forty-five minutes. The entire time, thoughts raced through my head: *What are they going to find? Is this another tumor? Surely this isn't cancer again. Lord, let it be just scar tissue.* After the MRI, I went back to the dressing room and checked my phone—Steve had left a message saying that he wouldn't be able to make it there in time, and to call him as soon as I was finished.

I sat down on the bench in the dressing room, afraid I was going to throw up. I was so scared my hands were shaking. After a few minutes, I took a deep breath and opened the dressing room door. Outside, a nurse was waiting to take me to the ultrasound room, a few doors down. Once again, they gave me a gown and asked me to change.

I changed, then sat and waited for the technician. It felt like déjà vu. This was, in fact, the same room I had sat in eight years before while I'd waited to have a mammogram that would forever change my life. *What if this isn't scar tissue?* I wondered. *What will they do? I hope this is nothing. Surely it's nothing. They've already taken most of the tissue. Please, God, don't let this be cancer again.*

The technician came back and led me into a dark room, where she told me to lie down, then rubbed warm gel over my right side. As she rubbed the wand over the gel on my side, the ultrasound machine beeped occasionally, the sound it makes when it takes pictures. I watched her face as she worked, and I could tell by her facial expression that something wasn't right. My heart started to beat faster. She put the wand down, then asked me to wait while she went to show the radiologist the pictures she had taken.

It took only a couple of minutes, but it felt like an eternity. I just lay there staring at the ceiling. *Is the cancer back? Why is this happening again?*

She came back in with a somber look on her face. "I've spoken with the radiologist," she said, "and she's concerned about the spot. She would like to do a biopsy."

"When does she want to do it?" I asked.

"She's on her way in now. We'll go ahead and take a sample before you leave."

While she was still speaking, the door opened and the radiologist came in. "Good afternoon, Sarah." She began to prepare her work area and equipment. "We're going to use this tool to extract a piece of tissue," she said, holding up something that looked like one of those guns they use in the mall to pierce your ears.

The ultrasound tech rubbed the wand over my side again until the area she wanted showed up on the monitor. The radiologist watched the screen, positioned the tool where she needed to make the extraction, then clicked it twice—and it was over.

"That's it?" I asked, surprised.

"Yep, that's it."

"That's a lot easier than the first biopsy."

"In the past several years," the radiologist said, "we've made a lot of advancements in our ability to extract tissue. Okay, we'll send this sample to the pathologist immediately. We should have the results within a day or two. I'll give you a call once we hear back."

As I cleaned off the gel and returned to the dressing room to change, I felt hollow and numb. I left the imaging center and headed toward the kids' daycare at church. Life wasn't going to stop to accommodate my anxiety. I took the kids home, fed them, and gave them baths. Steve and I went through the evening as usual; I didn't want to scare the kids, so I tried my best to keep a happy face, but inside I was scared to death. We had been down this road before, and we knew that obsessing over the unknown wouldn't help anyone. I tried to keep my mind distracted.

After the kids were in bed, I washed my face and got ready for bed myself. Steve and I lay in bed trying to watch the movie. I rested my head on his chest and he gently rubbed my hair. Neither of us spoke. His comfort and loving touch were all I needed. Finally I drifted off to sleep.

The next morning we hit the ground running with our normal routine. Steve took Colin to school; Tatum went with me. I dropped her off at daycare and headed downstairs to my office.

A couple of my close friends asked how things had gone at the doctor's. When I told them, they were as shocked as I had been. "We should hear something later today," I said.

I tried my best to concentrate on my work, but I found myself staring at the clock every few minutes, waiting for the phone to ring. It felt like an eternity, but finally noon arrived. I decided to get out of the office and ran to Target to pick up a few things for my Handbags of Hope.

"We received your biopsy results from the pathology lab. I have some hard news.
The results came back positive.
You have cancer. Again."

As I walked through the aisles at Target, gathering what I needed, I suddenly heard my phone ringing in the bottom of my purse. Adrenalin shot through my veins. I was in the makeup aisle—I had just picked up a bottle of vitamin E oil and dropped it into the basket. Frantically, I shuffled through my purse to find my phone. My hands were shaking, my palms sweating. I looked at the caller ID—*OK Breast Care.* My heart was about to jump out of my chest, it was beating so hard. *Here we go.* I took a deep breath and answered the call.

"May I speak with Sarah McLean," the woman said.

"This is Sarah," I replied.

"This is Doctor Gomez with Oklahoma Breast Care Center. I wanted to let you know—we received your biopsy results from the pathology lab. I have some hard news. The results came back positive. You have cancer. Interestingly, this isn't the same type of cancer you had the first time. This tumor is estrogen induced, unlike the first one. It's good that you continued doing self-exams, so we were able to catch it early. You'll need to make an appointment with a breast surgeon and your oncologist to determine a plan of action."

This isn't happening. I'm only thirty-four. It was as if she were speaking a foreign language that I couldn't understand. I didn't know how to respond. Eventually I mustered a thank you and asked for a referral to a breast surgeon, since my doctor had retired. She said that the nurse would call me back with the contact information. I clicked off the phone and put it back in my purse.

I had prayed and trusted God—and now I was right back where I started. *How could this be happening—again? Why? What are you doing, God?*

I was shaking. I just needed to get out of the store. I made my way through the checkout, and like a zombie I walked across the parking lot. Ironically, it was a gorgeous sunny day in August, no clouds in the sky. I found my GMC Yukon and unloaded the bags out of the cart. I climbed in and sat silently. As if in a dream, as if I were paralyzed, I just watched people walking to their cars in the Target parking lot. But it wasn't a dream. More like a nightmare.

I was in such shock I couldn't even cry. After a few minutes I mustered the energy to call Steve to tell him. *What would I say? How would he take the news?* I could tell by the tone of his voice that he was terrified, but he tried to stay as optimistic as he could—in an attempt to not discourage me, no doubt. He said that we would get through this storm as we had weathered every other storm.

I hung up and then sat in the Target parking lot for what seemed like hours. I closed my eyes and leaned my head back on the headrest. Tears began streaming down my face, and I cried out to God.

I don't understand! This makes absolutely no sense. I'm so tired of this being a part of my life. What are you doing? I know you're a good God. I know you're faithful. I know you're trustworthy. I know you can work all things together for my good, but I don't see how this can be good. Please help me. I need you now more than I've ever needed you. I can't do this without you. Be my strength.

His answer was a gentle whisper in my heart. *Sweetheart, I know you don't understand. In this life there will be situations and circumstances that you will be able to make sense of only when you meet me face to face. My ways are not your ways. My ways are higher than your ways. You said that you don't understand—but don't lean on your own understanding. Your finite mind isn't able to comprehend my sovereign ways. I need you to trust me. I have you in my hands. I have a purpose for you through this trial. I am your strength in the storm. Come to me. Rest in me.*

I decided to return to the office for the afternoon. I thought maybe I'd be able to distract myself with work. But as soon as I got back, my friends could tell something was wrong because my face was red and splotchy from crying. Slowly, word began to spread around the office. Several people came by to check on me. Surprisingly, they seemed to be more upset than I was. Maybe I was still in shock. Maybe I was in denial. Each person who tried to encourage me ended up crying and coming undone. Oddly, I was the one comforting them. And after a couple of hours of that, I was exhausted, so I decided to head home. I called Steve on my way, and he raced home to meet me.

Later in the afternoon I called the office of the breast surgeon the breast center had recommended. I made an appointment for the next morning. Tomorrow couldn't come quickly enough.

Steve and I decided not to say anything to the kids until we had a firm plan of action. Honestly, I had no idea what we would say once we did have a plan of action. That evening we decided to spend family time together. I wanted to bask in that quiet moment, knowing the mountain we were about to climb. We sat on the floor reading books to the kids. As I watched them, I wondered: Would I see my babies grow up? Would I get to see them graduate or get married? *This isn't fair to them,* I thought. *This isn't fair to Steve. They don't deserve to go through this. No one deserves to go through this.*

The next day Steve and I dropped the kids off and headed to the office of Dr. Rimes, the breast surgeon. *Here we go again,* I thought, checking in with the receptionist. Before long, the nurse escorted us to a room and I put on the hospital gown. Steve and I joked with each other, trying to lighten the mood as we waited.

A few minutes later, the door opened and a short man rushed in. His bubbly personality and bow tie made me smile. I liked him instantly. He was compassionate and kind. He took plenty of time to explain my options, and then he listened to my fears and concerns.

By the end of the appointment, we decided that he should try to do a lumpectomy and preserve the implant (if he removed it, I would have only one boob). He reminded me that he was just the surgeon, and that I would need to meet with my oncologist to determine the treatment plan. Just the thought sent a wave of fear through me. Would I need chemo? Radiation? Would it hurt? Would I lose my hair? Would I be well enough to take care of my babies? How would I manage all of this with kids? How could I do all this and work too?

Dr. Rimes said that he would like to schedule surgery as soon as possible. I agreed; the sooner we could get this out of my body, the better. We scheduled it for the following Tuesday.

Since we had a few days before surgery, Steve and I decided to take a short trip to Dallas. My mom and dad offered to watch the kids for us. We stayed in an ultramodern hotel and ate at some eclectic restaurants. We tried to have fun—which turned out to be harder than I'd expected. We took a walk one evening, but even that didn't dissipate the oppressive feeling that hung over us. We came upon a coffee shop and sat outside to sip our coffee. Neither of us spoke, but I'm sure that the same dark thoughts filled Steve's mind that filled mine. After a few minutes, I lost it and began to sob uncontrollably. Until then, I don't think I had allowed myself to truly grieve the diagnosis. I had tried to be stoic, to keep my game face on, to be positive. Sometimes it's better to just be real and honest. As cancer patients, we need to give ourselves permission to embrace and express our emotions as they come.

And what emotions had I been stifling and ignoring? I was angry, sad, scared, disappointed, confused—and most of all, I felt let down by God. This inner turmoil was waging war in my spirit. Steve gently caressed my hand. He didn't try to say anything to make it better. He knew I needed the freedom to allow my emotions to run their course. It took a half hour, but I finally felt a release inside. None of my questions had been answered, but I still felt a sense of indescribable peace. I had needed a moment like that—to just let it go—and I had allowed myself to have it.

What I discovered is that the more honest I was with myself about my feelings, the closer I felt to God. He was drawing me near. I began to sense a greater purpose with all this tragedy. Deep in my heart I believed that God would use these experiences, as unpleasant as they were, to reach people. I couldn't see his plan completely, but I knew that it was bigger than I could imagine. I believe the promise God gives us in Romans, where he assures us that he works all things together for the good of those who love him and who are called to his purpose. He is faithful, whether we're able to see it or not.

On Tuesday, August 9, 2011, Steve and I headed to the hospital early. My mom had stayed the night so that she could take the kids to their first day of school. It was Tatum's first day of kindergarten— and my heart was broken because I had been robbed of the opportunity to walk my baby girl into her classroom and help her get settled in and wish her a great first day of school. It wasn't fair. Cancer had stolen so many moments of my life. When would this end? How much is enough?

Once we got checked in, the radiologist used a needle to inject something into my side to mark the tumor, so Dr. Rimes would know the exact location once he started cutting. After they inserted the marker, we had to wait in the pre-op area for our surgery time. Steve kept me laughing. I was so thankful that he was lightening the mood. At about 9:00 that morning, Dr. Rimes came in with a chipper grin, wearing scrubs and his coke-bottle glasses.

"How are we this morning?" he said.

"Ready to get this over with," Steve said.

"No joke," I said.

"Then let's do this," the doctor said. "We should be in surgery for about an hour. I'll bring her back to post-op once she's finished."

Steve tenderly kissed my forehead and caressed my hand. "I'll be waiting for you."

Unfortunately, this whole scenario was all too familiar. I was worn out from all the surgeries. I prayed that we were on the home stretch.

I woke up in the recovery room. The nurse was feeding me ice chips. I asked her if I could see Steve. She went to find him. When he came in, he asked how I was feeling. I didn't feel much pain—the anesthesia hadn't worn off yet. He helped me get dressed, then wheeled me to the car in a wheelchair. When we got home, I tried to get some rest before the kids came home.

When Steve brought the kids home from school, they were so concerned. Both of them gently laid their heads on my stomach and softly rubbed my hand.

"Are you okay, Mommy?" they asked.

"Mommy is going to be fine. I'm just a little sore from the surgery this morning."

Their genuine, innocent concern was so thoughtful. But as I looked in their eyes, I wanted to sob—it just wasn't fair to them to see their mommy in this condition. But I held it together and encouraged them as much as I could. *No child should have to watch their parent go through this.* I was frustrated because, it seemed to me, a level of their innocence had been taken from them.

I tried to rest as much as I could, but it wasn't easy to stay down when I had two little ones and household responsibilities to take care of. After a week, I went back to work. A part of me felt that I had something to prove. I had already been through this once. I knew the ropes. I should be able to kick this with no problem. Right? What if people who would face the same thing someday were watching my response, looking to me to show them how they should respond? My need to control and perform was resurfacing. Why did I feel the need to prove myself?

It came back to haunt me. My first day back at work, I was in so much pain. The swelling on my side was getting worse instead of better, and the bruising was becoming darker. I called Dr. Rimes, and the next morning went to his office. He told me that I had developed a grapefruit-sized hematoma from doing too much too soon. I hadn't allowed my body enough time to heal, and the blood had formed a pocket inside and coagulated, so that it couldn't get out. Dr. Rimes suggested that we let it bleed out on its own, rather than cutting me open again. He told me to put hot compresses on the area several times a day, to break down the blood so that it could seep out.

So that's what I did—but it seemed to be taking much longer than I had hoped for the hematoma to bleed out. Four weeks later, the hematoma felt hot and was hurting excruciatingly. I asked my primary-care physician to take a look. Ironically, he hates the sight of blood. He needed only a glance at the area to know that it was infected. "We have to extract that blood," he said. I told him to do whatever he needed to—the pain was so bad I was in tears.

The nurse prepped me, and my doc slowly inserted the needle—blood began gushing out. The nurse put gentle pressure on the mass, and after thirty minutes, the swelling was gone. She had successfully removed all the blood. Now we had to wait for the infection to heal before I began radiation.

The radiation oncologist had recommended forty-eight treatments of high-dose radiation. The treatments would be administered five straight days, Monday through Friday. Each visit would last twenty minutes. We had decided to start as soon as possible. So by mid-September, with the infection under control, I was ready to begin.

The first day, I was nervous. I wasn't sure what to expect. Would it hurt? Burn? Steve was with me that morning. After I changed into a gown, I was escorted into a huge room with an enormous machine. Because of the radiation no one else was allowed in the room, so Steve waited outside with the technician in her booth and watched through the window.

Another tech told me to lie very still on the examining table. The machine would scan over the top of me. I would hear a beeping sound as the radiation was being administered. She asked me if I had any questions. I told her I was ready. She stepped out of the room.

I lay still and stared at the ceiling. It felt like I was in a dream. *I'm so tired of all this. Life is so unpredictable. We never know where we'll end up. I just want to move on with my life.* The ten minutes of treatment felt like an eternity to me, lying there. The door opened and the tech came back in to let me know we were finished. "You can get dressed," she said. "I'll see you tomorrow."

She did see me tomorrow, and the tomorrow after that. For the next six weeks, this became my normal routine. Drop the kids off at school and head to treatment. After treatment, come home and have coffee on my porch and spend one-on-one time with

Healing looks different for everyone.
For me, it meant drastically slowing my
lifestyle and making room to revel
in the presence of God and listen
for his whispers.

God. Sometimes listen to music or journal. Some days close my eyes and feel the cool breeze on my face and just sit quietly. I was pressing into him like I'd never done before. I wanted to have an intimate relationship with him, and now when my activities were sharply limited was the time to work on it.

As the weeks went on, my skin developed third-degree burns from the radiation. The outer layer of burnt skin on my right side sloughed off, leaving the new skin underneath wet to the touch. It wouldn't stop oozing. My doctor started giving me special wound care. The special gel bandages she gave me felt cool to the touch and provided some relief, but I was still in extreme pain. Even so, I continued to press on, both physically and spiritually. My physical strength was limited, but my emotional and spiritual strength was increasing.

Once again, I had to make decisions about my activities each day, hoping I was making the best decisions for my own rest and healing. This was no time to give in to my impulse to prove how strong I was, to show how I could "take it." I had already demonstrated that my tendency would be to put unnecessary pressure on myself to heal faster and get back to my normal routine. And I'm certainly not the first nor the only cancer patient who has struggled with this. We often feel the need to put on a "front," to show that we're okay, so that everyone around us will relax and stop worrying. As I showed at work, we take on the responsibility to comfort those around us, rather than comforting ourselves.

During those quiet times with God during my radiation treatment, he assured me that I had nothing to prove. He reminded me of the truths he had already instilled in my heart: *I am an individual. I am created in his image. I am unique and special. It doesn't matter what anyone else thinks I should do during this healing process. I'm the only one in a position to know.*

When we're on the outside looking in, we sometimes find it easy to judge others. It isn't until we've walked their journey that we can truly understand what choices we might make if we were facing similar circumstances. In my case, I needed to make the decisions that would hasten and encourage my own healing.

And what was best for me might not be the best choice for the next woman. Honestly, healing looks different for everyone. For me, it meant drastically slowing my lifestyle and making room to revel in the presence of God and listen for his whispers. For you, it might mean doing yoga, finding solitude, meditation, adopting a new method of eating, spending time with nature, spending time with family, exercising, or taking up a hobby you enjoy. Whatever your form of finding rest may be, it's crucial for you to discover. Allow yourself the space to explore. We must be gracious to ourselves through this process. It takes time to heal, so don't circumvent the process or you'll put yourself back at square one—and the process will take even longer.

We allow busyness to get in the way of our hearing God's voice. We become so consumed with *doing*, we forget to *be*. He just wants to be with us. He's not interested in what we can do for him. He loves us where we are, so it's okay for us to come to him just as we are—broken and helpless. We don't have to be cleaned up and whole for him to speak to us. But we do have to be available.

What if I told you to find a place of solitude, a place to get quiet and calm your mind? And once you'd found that space, suppose I asked you to just sit. Don't say anything. Don't do anything. How does that make you feel? Maybe the thought of that stillness and quiet makes you feel anxious. Maybe you think it sounds lazy or unproductive.

Ironically, that's exactly what God asks us to do. He asks us to come into his presence, to be still, and to allow him to fill our hearts. When we fully surrender our hearts, it gives God permission to take over.

What I discovered was that the more I invited him into my space, the more clearly I could hear his loving affirmations. He didn't expect me to have it all together. He didn't expect me to know how to deal with the roller coaster my life had become. He didn't judge me because I was still struggling. He simply loved me where I was, and by his grace I was ushered into his loving presence.

Come to me, sweetheart, he said. *I love you. I have good things for you. I know it's hard right now, but there is hope on the horizon. I know all things. Let me guide you. I am equipping you for my purpose.*

That's what he wants to do for you, too. If your journey through breast cancer and treatment has been a challenge, that's okay. You're not alone. We all cope in our own way. We simply come to him, and he will always be there with open arms, waiting for us.

When we allow the truth of God's promises to take up residence deep in our hearts, we begin to grow in spirit. Like a tree planted near water, our roots grow deeper and deeper, until they become so strong they can't be easily severed.

And as those roots develop, our faith grows. It's through his faithfulness that we become stronger. His goodness equips us. Even though we don't— and perhaps never will, until we stand before him in heaven—understand why we have to go through our cancer journey, God can give us the strength and patience to rise above this lack of understanding and trust him.

Chapter Eleven
A Day to Celebrate

The more time I spent with God, the more he shifted my heart in a different direction. To be honest, I had never wanted to be a stay-at-home mom or work from home, but God was gently nudging me. As I neared the end of my treatments, I thought about going back to work and about what our new normal would look like once again. Would I still be happy working outside of the home? What if I quit? How would that impact our family? And if I did, could I be a good stay-at-home mom? Would our family dynamics change for the better if I was more available? So many questions loomed as we neared the fork in the road.

On Tuesday, December 6, 2011, I dropped the kids off at school and headed to the hospital for my last radiation treatment. For the past six weeks, each morning, I had sat in this waiting room listening to the chatter of the other patients with the morning news playing on the TV in the background. I would peer at the small brass bell with a rope hanging from the clapper, hanging on the wall by the exit. When a patient completed their final treatment, they had the joyous honor of ringing the bell in celebration of their brave accomplishment. Now I sat there waiting for my name to be called one last time.

I had gotten to know the nursing staff well. Because I saw them every day, they had become like a second family. Kelly, one of my nurses, escorted me back to change. "Are you excited to be finished?" she asked.

"Excited is an understatement," I replied. And that was true—I couldn't wait to ring that bell and cross the finish line. But I also felt torn—things were changing. My *life* was changing. And I wanted something different.

"We're going to miss you around here. You're always so happy and full of joy," Kelly said.

I was so grateful to hear such kind words. "Wow, that's so nice of you to say. I'm going to miss seeing everyone too."

When the treatment was finished and I walked out of the treatment room, all the technicians were standing in a group, smiling. "Congratulations!" they shouted.

Tears streamed down my face as I hugged each of them and thanked them for their support and encouragement through this journey. It was a strange combination of gratitude and grief that I felt. I was grateful that they had walked this road with me, but now I would no longer see them daily as they cheered me on.

Before I left the dressing room, I stood in front of the mirror. Who was this new woman? Look how far she had come. No longer was she a weary, insecure, weak girl; she had blossomed into a strong, courageous, and passionate woman. I wiped my tears and smiled back at her. *You have a bright future, Sarah McLean!*

The celebratory bell hung on the wall near the exit door, waiting to be rung. I reached up, grabbed the rope dangling from the brass bell, and with a sense of profound accomplishment, I fiercely waved the rope back and forth. The sound echoed through the office. *I did it! I'm finished. I've won the battle.*

I turned and waved good-bye to the receptionists as they applauded. It was truly a triumphant moment, perhaps something like the elation of rock climbers when they reach the summit of a mountain. You've endured so many painful ups and downs along the journey—to finally reach the top is exhilarating and exhausting all at the same time.

I sat down in my car. Before I started it, I sat embracing the moment. Slowly I began to weep. I pulled a Kleenex out of my purse and gently wiped my face. As I slowly left the parking lot, I looked in my review mirror and thanked God this would be the last time I would be leaving as a patient.

When I got home, I put my purse on the kitchen counter and went to my bathroom to run a hot bath. I usually waited to take a shower until after my treatments, so I didn't smell like burnt flesh all day.

Today, though, I decided, was a day of celebration. I deserved a little "me" time. I took off my clothes and slipped into the hot water. When the tub was full, I leaned my head back, turned on the jets, and closed my eyes. The heat of the water soothed my body like a blanket covering me. The smell of eucalyptus bath salts filled the air. As I lay there soaking, my heart was overcome with emotion. I began to cry out to God.

Father, you know my heart. You know the path I've traveled. You know I've never wanted to stay home before, but I'm ready. Can I please come home and wholly devote my time to my family and to serving the breast cancer community through Project31? I know I haven't gone through all this crap for no reason. I know you've called me to be an advocate for breast cancer survivors and their families. Please let me do this! I want to obey you more than anything and I know you have a perfect timing for every season. I don't want to do it in my timing. I want to follow the flow of your Spirit. Is it time?

After I poured my heart out, I waited in silence with an expectant spirit. An overwhelming sense of peace washed over me. I heard no audible voice— just an internal assurance that I had his blessing to move on. I got out of the tub and dressed, filled with thoughts and questions about what was to come. I wanted to talk to Steve, but I was anxious about that conversation because I knew the sacrifice our family would have to make if I quit my job. *What would he think? How would we make it financially? What would I do for insurance? How would I feel if Steve didn't feel as I did about this?*

I sat outside on our front porch, where I normally went to calm my thoughts and get to a peaceful place. When I was ready, I picked up the phone and dialed Steve's number.

"Babe, I have something I need to share with you," I said.

"Is everything all right?" he asked.

"Everything's fine. I've just been thinking and praying a lot about our future now that I've finished my treatments."

"All right. And what have you been thinking?"

"Well, you know my heart has really been shifting since we've been going through treatment. I've really been burdened," I shared.

As I shared my heart with him—my increasing sense I should take the step of faith I'd been afraid to take and stay home to focus on our family and on building Project31—I became so overwhelmed with emotion he could barely understand what I was saying. "I'm ready," I said, finishing. "I believe it's time for me to quit working at the church. What do you think?"

Steve had patiently listened, allowing me to share everything I needed to say. Now it was his turn: "I know you've really been wrestling with what your new normal would look like," he said, "and

God is a God of new beginnings.
He's always making things new.
He likes to stretch us by allowing us to be
put into positions that may feel
uncomfortable. When we're walking into
the unknown, we have a choice:
trust him, or continue to try to control
everything ourselves.

what you really want to do moving forward. Now that you've finished your treatment, I think it's time to explore the direction for our future. Want to do some research on insurance options?"

"Okay," I said.

"Babe, I want you to be happy," he went on. "I know God has called you to reach the breast cancer community, so if it's time to take that step, I don't want to hold you back. If this is where God is calling us, then he will make a way."

"Thank you for being so understanding," I said, meaning every word. His support meant so much to me. I wanted us to be on the same page.

After we hung up, I called the American Cancer Society to see what kind of health insurance we would qualify for. They told me about a high-risk program funded by the state for cancer patients. I applied—and received a letter in the mail right before Christmas telling me I was *approved*. I was so grateful. God had made a way where there seemed to be no way.

Since I had worked at the church so long, I called my boss personally to let him know I was resigning before I contacted HR. It was a bittersweet conversation. We reminisced about everything we had walked through in my time working for him. We both cried. The past ten years of my life had been devoted to the church, but a new season was emerging. My heart was elated. I couldn't wait to see what God had in store.

❁ ❁ ❁

I believe God is a God of new beginnings. He's always making things new. He likes to stretch us by allowing us to be put into positions that may feel uncomfortable. When we're walking into the unknown, we have a choice: trust him, or continue to "try" to control everything ourselves. Those choices can provide spiritual breakthroughs. As God continues to take us into deeper levels of intimacy with him, we discover the more we let go, the more he's able to broaden our perspectives, open our hearts, and strengthen our level of influence.

To experience this, though, we have to be willing and able to transcend our routines. We tend to get comfortable with being comfortable. We don't like our schedules to be tampered with. Change can be scary. And inconvenient. To avoid the vulnerability of change, many of us just stay in the ruts. We become predictable. Life becomes boring. We stay in the safe and familiar rather than stepping into new spaces with God—until something like a cancer diagnosis blasts our world to pieces. Those times can be an opportunity to allow God to rock our world in the best way if we will allow him.

I believe we serve a courageous, adventurous, risk-taking God. He didn't die on the cross just to give us a safe, comfortable life—no risks, no chances, no adventure. He came so we can have life to the fullest, as he tells us in John 10:10. He wants us to step out by faith and trust his leading when he asks us to take a different path. The question is: Will we listen, believe, and obey?

Quitting my job to concentrate on the ministry of Project31—and raise my kids day by day—was a new path for me, and it was completely outside my comfort zone. But I knew without a shadow of doubt this was exactly where God had called me. He wanted to stretch me, to teach me something new. And he wanted to show me where I'd been wrong.

I had worked full-time outside the home since I was eighteen. Now I would be working *from* home. *What would my days look like? How would I organize my time? Would I be bored? Would I feel satisfied? Did I have the leadership capacity to build Project31? I didn't know how! How would this affect our finances?*

I had no idea how to be a stay-at-home mom! It was what I wanted, but I had no idea how to do it well. This would be a new adventure. For ten years I'd had the same morning routine: I would get up, get ready, get the kids ready, gather lunches and backpacks, and head to school. Now I had to find a "new normal." It took me a good six months to find a new rhythm. At first I didn't really know how to prioritize my time. I didn't know how to enjoy and maximize this newfound freedom.

I was learning day by day how to depend on the Father. My sense of inadequacy was heightened because I wasn't contributing financially to the family anymore. Instead, God was graciously reminding me he had been the provider all along. It had never had anything to do with me. My obedience was more important to him than the financial amount I personally contributed to the family's bottom line.

My journey with cancer was many things. For one, it was the avenue he was using to maneuver me into a place where I could rise up and encourage others.

I believe he extends toward each of us a unique and significant calling. To accept that calling, we must trust his leading for us and not doubt—or, even if we do doubt, we can still step forward in faith, despite our fears. Even though it might not seem that way to us, his timing is perfect.

In our case, stepping out in faith meant we made a financial sacrifice so I could quit my job. Not only did we lose my income, but we also gained the insurance expense. Not to mention the unending medical bills. *How would we make it?* The answer: God was continually faithful every month. Since we made the decision to step out and pursue Project31 full-time, our needs have always been met. I attribute that solely to God's faithfulness. He is trustworthy. He won't let us down. He always follows through with his promises.

Chapter Twelve
Back to Square One

Being at home was amazing. I loved being able to take the kids to school every morning and pick them up in the afternoon. I was thoroughly enjoying this newfound freedom and was so grateful for the opportunities God had given me to spend time one-on-one with survivors. Finally I had the margin in my schedule to go to treatment with other ladies or meet them for lunch to offer a word of encouragement. This new season was exhilarating.

Except for one thing: I began to experience twinges of pain on my right side. Honestly, I had grown accustomed to feeling slight discomfort. It's not uncommon to have residual pain after cancer, especially if you've had multiple surgeries and radiation therapy. In fact, when I finished my treatment, the radiation oncologist had warned me I would be at high risk for what is called *capsular contracture*, a common complication of breast reconstruction surgery. *Was I developing this condition?*

✿ ✿ ✿

Capsular contracture can cause your reconstructed breast to shift, change shape, or feel quite hard. Our bodies are smart—our immune system knows when a foreign object has been put within our tissues. When an intruder (such as an implant) is detected, a capsule made up of scar tissue forms around it.

Think of it this way: Our chest muscles and skin don't readily accept an implant as a natural part of our breast. In order to isolate the implant and keep it from growing, spreading, or wandering around, our body creates a sac, or capsule, of scar tissue around it, to seal it off. A capsule around a breast implant is naturally occurring tissue; it can benefit us. But if that capsule contracts or thickens, it can squeeze the implant. This contracture can cause severe pain, shifting, distortion, and hardening of the reconstructed breast.

✿ ✿ ✿

My radiation oncologist explained I might not have a problem, but she encouraged me to keep an eye on it. She went on to explain that if it began to cause pain, I would need to contact my plastic surgeon to address the issue before it became too much to bear.

Upon her recommendation I had been watching the scar tissue since I had finished my treatment at the end of 2011. Two years had passed by now and the scar tissue had gotten very thick and was squeezing my implant very aggressively, causing a lot of pain. Finally I decided it was time to call the plastic surgeon to see what was going on.

It had been ten years since I had been to my plastic surgeon's office. The last time had been in 2003 for the first implant reconstruction. A lot had changed. Most significantly, Dr. Shah's daughter, Bindu, had taken over his practice. She had a great reputation as a specialist in micro-vascular surgery. I had never met her.

As Steve and I walked into the office the receptionist greeted us. It felt like we were coming home. Most of the staff we knew were still there and were excited to catch up with us. We showed them pictures of the kids and told them what had been going on in our lives. It was comforting to be in a familiar place.

After Steve and I chatted with the ladies for a few minutes, we were escorted to an examining room to change. The nurse advised us Dr. Shah would be in shortly. I was eager to meet her.

The door opened and a short, spunky, young Indian woman walked in. She wore a leather skirt under her white jacket; a beautiful vine tattoo with tropical flowers wrapped around her leg. I liked her already.

She reminded me of her father. Her laugh, her smile, and her mannerisms resembled him in so many ways. Her sassiness was endearing—she wasn't the type to let anyone take advantage of her. As much as I liked her, though, I was completely unprepared for what she had to say.

After she examined me, she explained, "Radiation causes the skin to die. So if I removed the scar tissue, inserted a new implant and tried to sew you back up, the incision wouldn't heal. Basically what that means is, we'll have to take a flap of tissue from another part of your body to create a new blood supply."

Steve and I listened intently, but neither of us said a word. We were speechless.

"Usually we take a flap from the back or groin," she said. "It's your choice, but I think the latissimus-dorsi flap reconstruction would be the best option for you. The latissimus-dorsi muscle is located on your back, just below your shoulder and behind your armpit. It's the muscle that helps you do twisting movements. I will dissect an oval piece of tissue, fat, muscle, and blood vessels. I will transplant it to your breast. This is a very invasive surgery, so it's not a decision you should take lightly."

Steve and I looked at each other in disbelief. She could tell we were overwhelmed. "Why don't you and Steve go home and talk about it and call me once you've made a decision," she said.

Walking out of the office, I couldn't believe what I had just heard. I felt so defeated. *We have to go through more surgery? I thought. I'm tired of having my body mutilated. I thought we were finished with the residual effects of cancer. We've been walking*

*this road for ten years. How much more of my life is
this going to take up?*

From talking with other survivors, I already had
a good idea how invasive this surgery would be, and
I didn't want to endure the pain and go through
reconstruction all over again. I was pissed off. I had
already come so far. I didn't want to go backward.
Having another surgery felt like I was starting at
square one all over again.

✿ ✿ ✿

How much more of this do we have to go through?
I prayed. *How much more pain do I have to endure?
Yes, I know that I need to stay positive. I know you're
faithful. I know you're a good God, but I'm mad and
I need you to show me how I'm going to get through
this—and how you're going to use it, in my life and
the lives of others.*

Steve and I drove home in silence. The radio
was playing in the background, and I peered out the
window. Once we got home we had a couple hours
before we had to pick the kids up from school, so
we sat on our king-size bed, snuggled in the fluffy
yellow pillows, and had a long conversation about
our options. I told Steve we would just forget the
surgery—I would live with the pain. Better that, I
said, than to have half my back cut and my entire
chest reconstructed again. I didn't want to put Steve
through it again. I didn't want the kids to see me

in more pain. They had all been through so much already.

* * *

It was as if my life had become a never-ending horror movie. My heart ached. And I was scared. The surgery, if I decided to have it, would take seven to nine hours. I had never been under anesthesia that long, and the fear of overdosing again and not waking up haunted me. I would have to stay in the hospital for several days. There would be at least eight weeks of recovery, and the expansion process would take even longer to make room for the new implants. Not to mention the kids and their daily needs along with the household duties.

I couldn't stop crying. "I'm tired of being such a burden to our family!"

"Honey, you're not a burden to us. This is part of our life. You're in too much pain to go on as you are. I couldn't stand to see you live your life in this much pain. You *have* to have this surgery. We need you to be healthy. In the grand scheme of things, this will be a short-term pain for a long-term gain. It's part of the bigger picture for our family. You know God has a big plan for us. He's been faithful every step of the way. Have we liked all those steps? Of course not. But he has never let us down. And he won't let us down now."

"I know you're right. Thanks for allowing me to share my frustrations and fears. I know this is something we have to do."

We decided I would have the surgery in September of 2013. I had a couple of months to prepare mentally. It would be a *temporary* setback—but it would still be a setback, so I planned accordingly. By the time the day of surgery arrived, we had childcare set up. We had tons of friends signed up to bring meals. We had family and friends scheduled to stay with me while Steve was at work. I was as ready as I would ever be.

The morning of September 9, 2013, we had to be at the hospital at 6:00. We were the first surgery of the day. My heart raced as the nurse went through the paperwork with me and inserted my IV. In a little less than an hour I would be in surgery. The next thing I would be aware of would be waking up in tremendous pain. My only frame of reference was my double mastectomy. After that surgery, I had overdosed on morphine and stopped breathing. I kept taking deep breaths trying to calm my nerves. It felt like my heart was going to explode.

God, please don't let there be any complications. Allow the medication to work properly. Give the surgeon wisdom. Protect my babies as they worry about their mommy. Give Steve strength as we walk through this valley.

The anesthesiologist came into the pre-op room to explain the process. The lights were dim; I was snuggled under a stack of warm blankets. "Dr. Lawrence, I have to be honest. I'm pretty nervous about this surgery," I said. I told him about the situation after my double mastectomy.

"I'm so sorry that happened," he said. "But I assure you that won't happen today. I'll keep a close watch on you. I'll be there every step of the way."

Something in his voice—perhaps his confidence, perhaps his sense of compassion—made me believe him. This time would be different. An overwhelming sense of peace came over me.

`After he left, Steve and I sat quietly. "I love you, sweetheart," he whispered.

Then the nurse came to wheel me to the operating room. My hand brushed Steve's as I looked at him one last time. *God, please don't let this be the last time I see my husband or feel his touch.*

❖ ❖ ❖

Eight hours later I woke up in the post-op room, very groggy. I kept opening and closing my eyes, asking the nurse if I could see my husband. I have no idea what she replied—I was still mostly under the anesthetic—but I think she felt sorry for me so she snuck Steve back to my room. All I can remember was him holding my hand as I fell back to sleep.

Several hours later I woke up in my private room. To my surprise, I wasn't in as much pain as I had expected. "I want to see what it looks like," I told Steve, so he helped me pull the gown down;

underneath was a white compression vest with six drain tubes dangling from the bottom. "Holy crap!" I hadn't expected to bleed so much. I noticed a small ball of liquid similar to a drain tube dangling on the right side. Steve explained it was an anesthesia pump. It administers pain medication directly to the wound. It was incredible! That in itself was life changing. I couldn't believe how many advancements had been made in just ten years.

Unlike the first time, ten years before, I wasn't afraid to see the result, and the sooner the better. Gently, I unzipped the vest and removed the gauze. I couldn't believe how it looked. The mass of skin covered almost the entire right breast. I couldn't see my back because I was too sore to sit up at first.

I spent the next three days in the hospital. The nursing staff was amazing—so kind and helpful. They got me up and helped me walk the halls. So different from my previous experience—like night and day. I wouldn't have recovered nearly as well without them, and my heart was undone with gratitude to God. My family and friends had bathed me in prayer going into this surgery. Praise God! Those prayers were answered.

Because I did so well in the hospital, Dr. Shah allowed me to head home early. At home, I let the kids help me. They were so concerned. We didn't want to scare them with the unknown, so we let them be a part of the process. They helped me get dressed and drain the tubes. It was precious. My babies were growing in their compassion for others. Even though

I regretted they had to walk through this with us, I could see some sort of good coming from it already.

For the next four months, I visited Dr. Shah's office every two weeks for saline injections to stretch the new skin, just as I had in 2003. As those months passed, though, I noticed my breasts were becoming very uneven. *Had I gone through all of this to end up looking worse than when I'd started?* The thought made me sick.

We scheduled the reconstructive surgery for April of 2014. As Steve and I drove to the hospital that morning, my hope and prayer was that Dr. Shah would be able to correct the unevenness and give me a more symmetrical look. I tried to keep a positive mindset. After all, it wasn't as if I had anything more to lose, right? So this wasn't a vanity thing. It was a self-acceptance issue for me. We're women. It's not easy to lose our hair or our breasts. We were created with unique body parts that typify and express our female anatomy. When those body parts are damaged or taken away, it's hard to accept that reality. The grief never goes away. But we *can* learn how to recognize and manage our grief in a healthier way.

I came through the surgery with flying colors. There were no complications, and the pain was tolerable. Dr. Shah scheduled me to come in the morning after surgery to take out the drain tubes. I hadn't looked at the result yet.

It was a new facility and they weren't quite settled yet, so I had to ask the nurse to bring in a mirror so

I could take a look. I stood in front of the mirror, excited. Steve and my mom sat in chairs nearby, anxiously awaiting the "reveal." I unzipped the compression vest and gently removed the bandages. My heart was beating so fast.

I pulled open the vest—and I was devastated with the results. They weren't even. The implants had big, very visible ripples, and the skin flap made it look as if I were part of a patchwork quilt, or as if a pancake had been slapped on my chest. *What had gone wrong?* I didn't think I'd been expecting too much. I had known they wouldn't be perfect, but I would at least like them to be even.

As God continues to take us into deeper levels of intimacy with him, we discover the more we let go, the more he's able to broaden our perspectives, open our hearts, and strengthen our level of influence.

When would this end? How many low points would there be in this journey? Over and over, since my first diagnosis, I had felt like, as soon as I struggled to my feet, I was punched and knocked back down. Every morning after that, I woke up hating the way I looked. I knew I needed to speak up and ask the doctor what could be done to fix the problem. I had struggled so much in the past and had come so far to accept my new self. I knew I couldn't settle for a mediocre result this time.

A couple of days after surgery I mustered the courage to call the nurse. I had hesitated to call because I didn't want to be labeled a "high maintenance" or problem patient. However the reality was I am my best advocate, and if I wasn't happy with the results then I was responsible for speaking up. Through my tears I explained to the nurse how I was feeling about the results. She was so sweet and empathetic. She got me in right away to talk with the doctor. The doctor explained a couple of different options to me. Unfortunately, she wasn't very hopeful we would have a better result. I sat on the examining table sobbing. All the insecurities I thought I had worked through started to resurface. I had finally gotten to a place where I was comfortable with my body—and now, after this latest setback and surgery, I was back at square one. *Would I ever again be able to accept my body?*

I covered my face with my hands and cried a river of tears. I reassured the doctor that it wasn't her—I was just so tired. This journey had taken up so much of my life. *Why couldn't we just move on?*

Over the next couple of months I took inventory of my situation and my emotions, and I resolved to let these scars be my battle scars. I would concentrate on the fact I was alive. I wouldn't allow this setback to hold me down. I refused to fall into depression again. I wouldn't be a victim. I would hold my head high and continue living life to the fullest.

A couple months later it was a typical morning, I stepped out of the shower and dried off. I drew the towel away from my body and studied myself in the mirror. Then I noticed Steve was watching me look at myself. Neither of us spoke, but I could tell he knew how unhappy I truly was. Even if I had resolved to live with the results, how fair was that to my heart? He strongly encouraged me to get a second opinion. I resisted. I didn't want to be cut on again. I didn't want to endure any more pain.

After months of emotional pain, I relented. I made an appointment for a second opinion. What did I have to lose? I figured the doctor would confirm what I already knew—this was as good as it was going to get.

❊ ❊ ❊

Breast cancer is an assault on intimacy in marriage. This disease can steal not only our femininity but also our ability to accept ourselves. It can drive a wedge between us and our partners. Our husbands were created to be our protectors, lovers, and leaders. They long to keep us safe and resolve any problem that presents itself in our lives. Unfortunately, husbands can feel crippled when it comes to breast cancer. Their instincts tell them to do something, to save us, to be our protector—but they don't know how. They often feel helplessly sidelined.

I'm thankful that Steve accepts me just the way I am. It isn't my physical attributes that captivate him—it's my heart. Sadly, I've met so many women who aren't able to say that. The men in their lives struggle desperately with the woman's disfigurement and their inability to fix or control the situation.

Steve is a different breed … in more ways than one. (Ha!) He's one in a million, he's mine, and I'm grateful every day to have such a warrior by my side. His love, patience, loyalty, and tenacious spirit have saved me more than once through these battles. We've gone through many storms that we would never have made it through without each other. Because of that, we are passionate about seeing God heal marriages. We know that marriages can survive this fire of cancer, because ours has. We want to see the marriages of others be, as ours is, stronger and more empowered on the other side of this trial.

※ ※ ※

The plastic surgeon we'd chosen for our second opinion was kind and informative. To our surprise, he had a laundry list of suggestions to improve my look. I was blown away. I frankly hadn't expected him to have any ideas we hadn't already heard, so I was pleasantly surprised. He agreed to work with us, and for the first time since the previous surgery, I dared to hope these flaws could be repaired.

He said, "I want you to be able to go to the beach and have no one know you've ever had breast cancer."

"That's exactly what I want!"

We sat down with his office manager to see when he might be available. My current insurance policy was dissolving on December 31, 2014, and I had already met my deductible. It was already the end of September, so we needed to move fast.

"He's already booked until the end of the year," she said. "But I just got a call from a patient canceling a surgery for next week."

Steve and I looked at each other. We knew what we had to do. The timing was certainly unexpected, but we were both confident God was presenting us with an opportunity. I looked at her and said, "Let's do it."

Over the next couple of days, I made arrangements for the kids, had the house cleaned, and bought extra groceries. Unfortunately, we had become old hands at this surgery thing.

On October 1, 2014, we arrived and checked in. The nurses prepped me for surgery at lightning speed. I had never had a hospital entry go so fast and smooth. The operating room was very bright. The staff was energized and ready to go; '70s rock was playing in the background. The doc came in and joked, "Have a nice nap. We'll see you in five hours." I closed my eyes and off to sleep I went.

The doctor did what they call "fat graftings." He sucked fat from my stomach and back and injected it into my chest to give better projection and a symmetrical natural look.

I thought I knew what pain was ... little did I know. When I came out of surgery, the pain was excruciating. Jamming a metal rod in and out of your abdomen a thousand times causes a little discomfort. While I slowly healed over the next six weeks, I wore an insanely tight compression garment that supported my torso and kept my body molded. I would massage the muscles and move the fluid to the lymph nodes so I didn't develop lymphedema.

Despite the pain, I was very happy with the results—elated, actually. I couldn't have asked for a better outcome. I was overjoyed. I wouldn't have even thought it was possible. Thank God that Steve was insistent on my getting a second opinion.

One of the hardest things for patients is to question the performance or the counsel of our medical teams. We feel a sense of loyalty to them. Even so, we are our own best advocates, responsible for our own choices. After all, we're the ones who have to live with the results. If we're not happy with something, or don't understand the terminology, or don't have inner peace about the direction we're being led, then we must stand up for ourselves. Ask questions. Speak to other survivors about their experiences to get a patient perspective. No one knows our bodies like we do. We must speak our minds and not settle for second best.

You have a voice in your own medical treatment. It deserves to be heard. It must be heard.

Chapter Thirteen
A New Chapter

Ten days after my surgery I had been invited by the pastor of a local church in Oklahoma City—a close friend of ours—to share my story at his church's annual women's conference. The theme was "Being a Woman of Strength."

I was honored and humbled to be asked—but also nervous, once again, about speaking in front of people. Still, I knew I needed to do it. I had to lean into my fear and trust God's leading. I emailed my friend and told him I would gladly be a part of the conference.

As soon as I'd sent the email, I went to the conference website and looked at the list of other speakers. The keynote speaker was Lisa Bevere, an author and international speaker and an amazing woman of God. Her heart for women is so inspiring. She and her husband, John, have been doing international ministry for twenty years. I was humbled I would be in the presence of such an inspiring woman.

I had heard Lisa speak for the first time just two years before at the same conference. At the time, she had just released her book *Lioness Arising*, in which she inspires women to awake from their slumber and walk in the magnificent image of strength, passion, and beauty. She challenges us to rise up in God's strength and change our world.

That book forever changed my life; her passion and authority bled off the page. Her words gave me a new confidence. Now it was time to put that confidence to the test. I *must* engage in the battle. I *must* raise my sword. I *must* fight to proclaim the freedom God sacrificially died to give all of us.

The day of the conference arrived. I couldn't wait—how exciting to be part of such a powerful time of women coming together and seeking God, comforting one another and rising in their God-given strength. As I sat in the green room going over my notes, Lisa sat down to eat her breakfast beside me; her kindness and her interest in getting to know me spoke volumes. She was humble and down to earth. Even though she had preparation to do, she took the time to encourage me and build me up. She had never met me before, but she took that moment to breathe life into me.

Suddenly I could hear the band begin to play. It was time to go into the auditorium. I followed my friends out to the front and we sat down. As worship ended, my friend Jon greeted the ladies and introduced me. Before I stepped onto the stage, we rolled a video of the testimony I had produced for my website. As the video ended, the ladies stood and cheered. I was so humbled, but on the strength of their response I approached the stage with confidence. I took a deep breath and walked up the steps, praying, *God, this is all you. Please use me to bring glory to you. Not in my strength, but through your strength within me. I pray the story you are telling in my life is an encouragement to all these women today. May they be renewed and inspired with a fresh hope.*

There were two cozy, high-back chairs on stage, and over the next twenty-five minutes, Jon and I sat and had a conversation. Honestly, I don't remember a lot of what was said. It wasn't me. It was God speaking through me. Passion overflowed from my heart, and tears streamed down my face as I exposed some of the most intimate struggles of my life. God was breathing life and hope through me to these broken women. It didn't feel like I'd had time to blink before the session was over.

As we finished, the ladies stood and cheered. I bowed my head and wept. I was so humbled and overwhelmed by their response. *Who was I to be honored in this way?* God is so good. He desires to use all of us in a unique and special way. All we have to do is say yes.

※ ※ ※

We must open our mouths and empower
women to rise from their brokenness
and not allow their circumstances to
determine their lives.

That day at the women's conference was a key event for my future. I left the church that day with my heart overflowing with love for these women. I yearned for more opportunities like that to share my story and offer hope to broken souls. It was the beginning of a new chapter in my life.

God is a magnificent storyteller. He's continually writing our stories. No matter what we're going through in life, we are a reflection of him. We are his workmanship. The good news for us as cancer survivors is that our stories don't have to end with cancer. Cancer doesn't define us. It's only part of our story. How will God continue to use the messiness of cancer for good in our lives?

All of us can relate to hardships, whether we've ever been diagnosed with cancer or not. Trials will come. There will be storms in life. They're inevitable. They're part of the story.

God doesn't try to deceive us by sugarcoating the reality of life. He *clearly* tells us up front we will have troubles on this earth (John 16:33). The good news is our Savior died a sacrificial death to give us forgiveness, healing, restoration, peace, and fullness of life. In other words, we weren't created to merely exist. We were created to give hope to the world. Our stories are a beacon of hope to the women who lie on the battlefield wounded.

The question is, Will we allow our tragedy to consume us? Or will we rise above the storm of cancer by fully surrendering our situation, feelings, circumstance, doubts, fears, and insecurities to Christ, accepting his gift of salvation and believing his promises? He is our anchor in the storm. He won't let us fall. He will sustain us. He will carry us. Not long after my reconstructive surgery, Steve and I sat down for a dedicated time of asking God to show us where he wanted us to go. How did he want us to move forward with Project31? What was the next step? Where were we going?

As we sought God's plan, he started to open doors in miraculous ways. A mustard seed of faith to take him at his word is all he asks. As we continued drawing near to him, he drew near to us. Step by step he was guiding us.

After years and years of fighting, pain, hurt, and despair, I finally relinquished control of my life to him, in the belief that he would restore everything that had been stolen from me. His Word tells us in Revelation 21:5 that he is making all things new.

A righteous anger ignited in my soul. I could not idly stand by, watching cancer destroy more lives. We are in a *war*, ladies. We have a job to do, and that job will require all of us to join forces as a unified army of fierce soldiers. We must rise up as women of God, as warriors. We must fight.

We can't allow cancer to gain any more ground. We can't allow more women to be assaulted, more marriages to be destroyed, the innocence of any more children to be stolen. *We must open our mouths and empower women to rise from their brokenness and not allow their circumstances to determine their lives.*

For me, that meant it was time to build Project31. Time to jump into the deep end of the pool. No more holding back. This was serious business, and I needed to be all in. Was I ready for the challenge? How much did I really know about running a nonprofit? I just want to love people. I just have a dream to see women healed and hearts restored.

One of Steve's mentors whom he hadn't seen in a long time came to my mind. His wife was CEO of a local nonprofit. I thought it might be a good idea to sit down with her and profit from her experience. Steve connected us and we set up a coffee date.

Joanna had built, from the ground up, what is now a multimillion dollar organization. I was intimidated just to chat with her! But as the two of us sat in IHOP, drinking our coffee and letting our breakfast get cold, she quickly put me at ease with her warm smile and cheerful demeanor.

"Tell me your story," she said. "I know bits and pieces, but I want to hear the whole thing."

"Do you have all day?" I joked. "I don't want to take up all the time."

She listened intently as I poured my heart out. Her smile and reassuring nods showed me she understood my passion. At the end of that first meeting, I asked if she would consider mentoring me. I knew it was critical to have a coach, cheerleader, and biggest fan if I was going to build Project31 into a sustainable business.

I wasn't sure what she would say. She was a busy woman with a lot on her plate. But after considering it, she agreed.

Over the next couple of months, we met regularly. I would give her reports on my progress and she would guide me about the next steps. Under her mentoring, I was gaining confidence in my ability to step out in faith and truly walk in the calling I believe God has called me to. God equips those he calls, and he empowers those he equips. I could do this. I could lead Project31. Not in my own strength, but in God's strength. The more I leaned into God and his heart, the bigger my dreams grew.

Hope rises when we see each other face the trials of life with courage and bravery and come out stronger on the other side.

One of my dreams for Project31 was to expand our support groups to other local hospitals. Steve and I met with the president of the Integris Cancer Institute of Oklahoma where we started our first group. He was overjoyed with our vision to develop a sustainable and healthy support group model. He had already witnessed the success of our group, so he knew we would follow through in a healthy way. God was giving us favor. Within three months of that conversation, we had launched another group, with future plans to launch more groups.

During one of our coffee dates, Joanna suggested I meet with her husband; she thought his expertise in the business sector would be helpful. His name is Michael, but most people call him Smitty. He specializes in mentoring CEOs. My first meeting with him, a couple of days later, left me feeling so challenged and inspired I asked him if he would mentor me in building a business. He graciously agreed. Once again, God was giving me undeserved favor.

When we say "yes" to his call, he will make a way where there seems to be no way; people will come alongside us to join in the adventure. God doesn't expect us to do this life alone. We're only as strong as our support system. I was so grateful for the time Joanna and Smitty were investing in me. Every time I met with them, I grew more and more as a leader. For the first time, I was confident I was capable of obeying God and following through with the destiny he has for me.

In order to continue moving forward, I needed to raise financial support. It's not easy to ask for money, but God started bringing people to mind—people Steve and I had personal relationships with who had watched us walk through this journey, people who believed in God's call on our lives. As I began sharing our vision with them, God astonishingly started to flood us with resources even beyond our expectations. I was being blown away by the wonder of God. I never would have dreamed he would do this for me. But he has—and he will do amazing things for you too.

I have big dreams for Project31. One day I want to partner with cancer institutes all over the nation to build restorative centers where cancer patients and their families can come for counseling, yoga, massages, medical spa treatments, nutrition, and integrative therapy. The sky is the limit with God. He knows no boundaries. Nothing is impossible to him. *Nothing.*

I've shared with you a lot of intimate details of my journey with cancer in this book. Why did I? Because I think it's necessary for us to be real. To be vulnerable. *Hope rises when we see each other face the trials of life with courage and bravery and come out stronger on the other side.* We need each other.

What's the next chapter of *your* story?

Only God knows the future, and I don't know where Project31 will be in ten years. All I know is, when you're following the guidance of the Holy Spirit, each day is a new adventure filled with excitement and uncertainty.

God's not finished with me yet. He's not finished with you.

The story's not over....